PAUL: MOULDED BY HIS MESSAGE

The *Character and Charisma* series introduces us to people in the Bible and shows how their lives have much to teach us today. All the authors in the series use their communication skills to lead us through the biblical record and apply its encouragements and challenges to our lives today. Every volume contains an *Index of Life Issues* to enhance its usefulness in reference and application.

Other books in the series

Elijah: Anointed and Stressed by Jeff Lucas
Elisha: A Sign and a Wonder by Greg Haslam
Gideon: Power from Weakness by Jeff Lucas
Joshua: Power to Win by Kevin Logan
Mary: The Mother of Jesus by Wendy Virgo
Moses: The Making of a Leader by Cleland Thom
Samson: The Secret of Strength by Phil Stanton
Esther: For Such a Time as This by Jill Hudson

CHARACTER AND CHARISMA SERIES

Paul
Moulded by His Message

CHARLES PRICE

KINGSWAY PUBLICATIONS
EASTBOURNE

ISBN 0 85476 850 5

Published by
KINGSWAY PUBLICATIONS
Lottbridge Drove, Eastbourne, BN23 6NT, England.
Email: books@kingsway.co.uk

Designed and produced for the publishers by
Bookprint Creative Services, P.O. Box 827, BN21 3YJ, England.
Printed in Great Britain.

Contents

Introduction 7
1. Drama on the Damascus Road 9
2. Profile of a Convert 21
3. Motivated by Vision 37
4. Time Out with God 55
5. The Value of a Friend 69
6. Finding and Doing the Will of God 81
7. A Strategy for Evangelism 97
8. Restoring Righteousness 113
9. Facing Foolish Christians 127
10. Union with Christ 139
11. Civil War in the Soul 151
12. The Strength of Weakness 167
13. Learning the Secret of Being Content 177
14. Passing the Baton 193
Study Guide 207
Selective Bibliography 215
Index of Life Issues 217

Introduction

Apart from Jesus Christ, it is safe to say that no person has had a greater impact on the past 2,000 years of Christian history than the apostle Paul. His letters comprise 13 of the 27 books of the New Testament and his personality dominates the landscape of the early church and the subsequent two millennia of its history.

This book is not a biography of Paul as such, for much more able writers have given us several of those in recent years, not least John Pollock's recently republished work, *Paul the Apostle*,[1] and Professor F.F. Bruce's magnificent work, *Paul: Apostle of the Free Spirit*.[2] Any feeble attempt by me to add to these would be pointless. My prime concern is not so much with the unfolding drama of Paul's life, but more with discerning the fire that burned in the apostle's heart and permeated his ministry.

This book, therefore, is a manual on the Christian life, seen primarily through the lens of Paul's experience of God, but fleshed out to some extent against the wider background of the experience of others in the Scriptures with whom Paul stands in a long and harmonious line. Nothing about Paul's passion for Christ, his understanding of the gospel, and the sense of his

---

[1] Kingsway Publications, 1999.
[2] Paternoster Press, 1977.

complete dependency on God should be regarded as unique to him. He writes boldly, 'Whatever you have learned or received or heard from me, or seen in me – put it into practice. And the God of peace will be with you' (Philippians 4:9). In other words, 'You live as I have lived, and the God you have seen in me will be equally evident in you.' What was true for Paul may be true for us, as we too learn to enjoy the rich relationship with Christ that Paul so demonstrably had.

So what was his passion? He perhaps expressed it best when in his letter to the Galatians he described himself as being like a mother giving birth: 'My dear children, for whom I am again in the pains of childbirth until Christ is formed in you' (Galatians 4:19). This was the sublime end to which everything Paul said and did pointed – the forming of Christ in people. It had begun in his life on the Damascus road when 'God, who set me apart from birth and called me by his grace, was pleased to *reveal his Son in me* so that I might preach him among the Gentiles' (Galatians 1:15–16, my emphasis). God not only revealed his Son *to* Paul on that dramatic day, but he began the process of revealing his Son *in* Paul. This is the ultimate goal of the Christian life, 'For we who are alive are always being given over to death for Jesus' sake, so that *his life* may be revealed in our mortal body' (2 Corinthians 4:11, my emphasis).

Paul was Christocentric, and we dare be nothing less if we too are to know in our experience the same divine resources that were demonstrated in his life. Though in different bodies, with different personalities, in a different age, and in a hugely different world, that remains the goal.

My prayer as you read these pages is not that you know Paul better, but that through the apostle Paul you may know Christ better, and find that to know him is to know life in its fullest expression.

Charles Price

1

Drama on the Damascus Road

Some things are indelibly fixed in our memories. I remember the day I was chased by a wild elephant while on a visit to southern India. Leaping into a river in my attempt to get away, my splash gave the elephant such a shock, it turned around and ran off in the opposite direction. The local people were suitably impressed and gave me a nickname meaning 'The one of whom elephants are afraid'! I don't know about the elephant – all I know is that I was terrified!

I remember also my wedding day and the birth of each of our three children. Moments like these stick in our memories as life-changing events.

There was one event fixed indelibly in the mind of the apostle Paul. It became the foundation of everything he came to be, and a story he was to tell repeatedly. When he awoke on that morning it was the last and least likely event to be expected. But it happened. In the full light of the Middle Eastern noonday sun, as he approached the city of Damascus, suddenly a light, much brighter than the sun above, flashed around him. Saul of Tarsus and his travelling companions from Jerusalem fell to the ground in fear, when from the blazing light Saul heard a voice in his own Aramaic tongue calling him by name, 'Saul, Saul, why do you persecute me?' (Acts 26:14). That moment changed for ever the life of this brilliant young leader of men.

Traditional wisdom tells us that a man with an experience is more powerful than a man with an argument. Saul of Tarsus (whom we will now call by his better known Latin name *Paul*, rather than his Jewish name *Saul*) studied for years under Gamaliel, the most prestigious teacher in Jerusalem, to become a Pharisee. During this time he was exposed to all the arguments presented by the leaders of the new radical movement known as 'The Way', which was turning Jerusalem on its head and threatening the stability and security of the Jewish traditions. With his razor-sharp intellect he had tried to rebuff the arguments, and the debates he had with members of the new movement, far from convincing him of the credibility of their position, had only served to harden his resistance and increasingly fanatical opposition to anyone who dared advocate these ideas.

The Way had been founded on the teachings of an uneducated itinerant Galilean preacher. This man not only claimed to be the Son of God, but his followers ludicrously affirmed this claim to have been vindicated by his resurrection from the dead three days after suffering brutal crucifixion under Roman law outside the city walls of Jerusalem, not more than three years before Saul's encounter on the road to Damascus. There were plenty of rational and circumstantial reasons for Saul to disbelieve this story, not least the evidence given by the soldiers who were guarding the tomb on Pilate's orders that they had unintentionally fallen asleep during the night of the claimed resurrection, giving opportunity for some of the disciples of Jesus to come and steal the body away. Saul had no reason to know that the soldiers had been generously bribed by the chief priests and elders of the Jewish community to make this allegation, nor would he know that the governor himself,

Pontius Pilate, had been persuaded not to take action against the apparent negligence of his soldiers. Thus it was that this officially unchallenged evidence had circulated for the past three years or so around Jerusalem, and would continue for many years yet as the most plausible explanation for the empty tomb (see Matthew 28:12–15). In any case, the nondescript band of people who comprised the membership of this new movement, many of whom were now living off shared resources in a form of community living, undermined by their social and economic status the credibility of their claim to have recognized in Jesus the long-awaited Messiah. Surely it would be the prerogative of the educated and ruling classes to whom Paul belonged to pronounce that judgement.

But all of his presuppositions and conclusions changed in little more than a twinkling of an eye under the midday sun close to the boundaries of the great city of Damascus. Paul experienced something that day which no apologist, no preacher, no humble believer and no apostle could ever create for themselves. He encountered the risen and still living Christ, who revealed himself unambiguously, calling this young Pharisee by his own name.

Such a dramatic encounter with the risen Christ appears to most of us as unfair! Interestingly, just as I was writing this chapter, one of the students in our Bible school put his head around my study door and asked if he could talk with me for a few minutes. He told me he had been a Christian for years, but was concerned about the quality of his experience of God. It just wasn't very dramatic or exciting. He had been talking with a fellow student who was dramatically converted to Christ on the streets of Amsterdam, came off drugs, turned around from a completely amoral lifestyle, and now has a relationship with Jesus Christ that is alive, exciting and contagious. He asked me whether it might have been better if he had sinned a bit earlier on, got himself into real trouble, and then come to Christ so that the changes would be so much more dramatic and therefore much more obvious and real to him. After all, his family were Christians, he had understood the gospel from boyhood, he had been secure and never felt the need to rebel. Was he missing out?

There is something about the dramatic conversion that is so much more convincing, but what had Saul of Tarsus done to make him worthy of such an experience? He had risen to become the arch-enemy of the newly developing church. His name first occurs in Scripture as the young man who, though too young to participate legally in the stoning of Stephen, had stood on the sideline and enthusiastically encouraged the brutal and bloody death of one of the brightest lights in the infant church of Jerusalem. Surely he, of all people, didn't deserve to get converted.

Paul was a contemporary of Stephen, having arrived in Jerusalem from Tarsus for a second visit only shortly after the death and resurrection of Christ. It is unlikely Paul was in Jerusalem at the time of Jesus, for he makes no reference either to hearing Jesus or to confronting him as other Pharisees did. His zeal for the law, and opposition to everything that undermined it, meant he almost certainly would have confronted Jesus had he met him. Nor does Paul claim to have been present at the crucifixion, as he surely would have been had he been in the city at the same time, knowing his strong fanatical opposition to Jesus. It is most likely therefore that Paul had spent his five or six years learning at the feet of Gamaliel in Jerusalem prior to Jesus' ministry there, and had then gone home to Tarsus. If Paul had ambitions to become a member of the Sanhedrin Council, a body of 71 elders presided over by the high priest in Jerusalem, who were the supreme authority in religious affairs and who exercised the minimal self-government Rome permitted the Jews, then he was required to complement his academic training in law with a practical trade by which he could provide for himself. He chose tent-making as his trade, which served him well in years to come (see Acts 18:3), and probably returned to Tarsus in Cilicia, some 550 miles from Jerusalem, to learn the trade and do his apprenticeship.

Paul's wife?

If this reconstruction is accurate, then Paul returned to Jerusalem in the years immediately following the ascension of Christ. Whether he came with a wife or not we do not know, but it is highly likely that he was married at some stage. Not to marry and have children once a young man came of age was exceptionally rare, and marriage was a compulsory requirement for membership of the Sanhedrin, should Paul have held ambitions in that direction. What is clear, however, from his own writing is that during the years of his apostleship he lived as a single man, though, as he pointed out, other apostles like Peter and James took their wives with them on their missionary travels (1 Corinthians 9:5). Paul advocates the benefits of celibacy when he writes to the Corinthians, 'Now to the unmarried and the widows I say: It is good for them to stay unmarried, as I am' (1 Corinthians 7:8). He appears to hold a rather cynical (some might say realistic) view of marriage when he goes on to say, 'But those who marry will face many troubles in this life, and I want to spare you this' (verse 28).

We can only speculate about Paul's marital status earlier in his life. Was he a widower, whose wife had died early on, perhaps leaving him childless? This is certainly possible, though the memories of those who have lost a loved wife or husband usually grow fonder with passing time and are

positive. In contrast, memories of broken marriages are associated with the hurts and disappointments that broke the marriage and tend to be more negative. Is it possible that behind
this apparent cynicism of marriage lies a sad and painful experience that Paul had endured? He treats very compassionately
the dilemma faced when one partner in a marriage becomes a
Christian and the other does not and the unconverted partner
wishes to leave:

> And if a woman has a husband who is not a believer and he is
> willing to live with her, she must not divorce him . . . But if the un-
> believer leaves, let him do so. A believing man or woman is not
> bound in such circumstances; God has called us to live in peace.
> (1 Corinthians 7:13–15)

Could it be that Paul was married to a woman who did not
welcome his conversion on the Damascus road, who was
perhaps ambitious for her husband with his intellectual powers
and leadership skills to go to the very top of Judaism, but now
that he had been converted to Jesus Christ – whom together
they may previously have opposed – could no longer remain
with him? It is certainly possible. In giving testimony to the
Philippians of his renunciation of all he had previously held
dear, for the 'surpassing greatness of knowing Christ Jesus my
Lord', he adds, 'for whose sake I have lost all things'
(Philippians 3:8). Did his loss of 'all things' include a wife and
perhaps even a family? We cannot know for sure, but it is legitimate speculation.

When Paul first enters the biblical story, however, he has
returned to Jerusalem from Tarsus, whether with a wife or not,
and is ready for the fight against the followers of Jesus Christ,
which is already growing into a major battle. Shortly after the
ascension the apostles had been brought before the Sanhedrin,

where Paul's teacher Gamaliel had advocated the more passive and patient approach of leaving them alone:

> For if their purpose or activity is of human origin, it will fail. But if it is from God, you will not be able to stop these men; you will only find yourselves fighting against God. (Acts 5:38–39)

Clearly Paul disagreed with his mentor and felt it was dangerous to leave the Christians alone, so he set himself to participate in stopping them.

The martyrdom of Stephen drew the line in the sand Paul had been hoping for. Stephen was one of the greatest orators in the infant church, so much so that when members of the Synagogue of the Freedmen, Jews of Cyrene, Alexandria, Cilicia and Asia (Paul was almost certainly one of those listed from Cilicia) confronted Stephen, 'they could not stand up against his wisdom or the Spirit by whom he spoke' (Acts 6:10). This group of men persuaded others to claim they had heard Stephen speaking words of blasphemy against Moses and against God. It would be only a matter of time before the showdown, and it came with the mob rule that illegally encouraged Stephen's accusers to throw the heavy, jagged stones that quickly ended his life and left his body an unrecognizable obscenity of mangled flesh, blood and bones.

The martyrdom of Stephen only seemed to enhance Paul's taste for blood. He was no doubt part of the great persecution that broke out against the church at Jerusalem following Stephen's murder, and not satisfied with that, followed the dispersing church to wherever they thought they might find a safe haven, 'breathing out murderous threats against the Lord's disciples' (Acts 9:1). In his obsession he began to tour foreign cities in order to root out and persecute any followers of Jesus Christ, convinced he ought to do all that was possible to oppose the name of Jesus. Now Paul's reputation as an effective persecutor of believers in Jesus had become a catalyst for motivating other like-minded opponents to join the fight. He sought with growing venom to channel their anger in constructive strategies to destroy this threat to the purity of Judaism once and for all, and could hardly open his mouth without spitting outrage against anyone daring to be a disciple of Jesus Christ.

It was not reckless guerrilla warfare in which he engaged – he was too clever for that. He made his activities part of the official policy of the Jewish hierarchy, rather than be accused of acting on his own whim:

> He went to the high priest and asked him for letters to the synagogues in Damascus, so that if he found any there who belonged to the Way, whether men or women, he might take them as prisoners to Jerusalem. (Acts 9:1–2)

With legal status for his murderous activities Paul rounded up his gang of supporters for the 150-mile journey from Jerusalem to Damascus, complete with all the equipment necessary to arrest, chain and drag his victims back to Jerusalem. But he never reached Damascus. At least, the murderous Saul of Tarsus never arrived! The man who entered the city gates turned up in the same body as the man who had left Jerusalem, but instead of the murdering antagonist of Jesus Christ, he arrived with a description given him by God as 'my chosen instrument' (Acts 9:15). This was a remarkable occurrence – something had happened on the road outside Damascus that left Saul of Tarsus a completely transformed man.

The details are well known. After the bright light had blazed around and Paul had heard the calling of his own name, he replied, 'Who are you, Lord?' To his utter amazement the reply came back, 'I am Jesus, whom you are persecuting . . . Now get up and go into the city, and you will be told what you must do' (Acts 9:5). The men travelling with Paul stood there speechless; they heard the sound, but did not see anyone, nor could they discern the words that were so clear to the ears of Paul. He got up from the ground, but when he opened his eyes he found he could see nothing. It was not the brightness of the light that had blinded him, for his companions suffered no such ill effect, but a miracle of God. The physical sensation of surrounding blackness mirrored the darkness and confusion of Paul's own inner self. Three days later this would be repealed under the hands of Ananias in Damascus, symbolizing too the freedom and enlightenment that would accompany the coming of the Holy Spirit to indwell him. Paul's companions led him by the hand into Damascus.

It is the seeming suddenness and drama of Paul's encounter with Jesus that doesn't seem fair. There are people we would love to become genuine Christians, who, if only they could experience something as dramatic as this, would surely realize the truth of the gospel and submit themselves to Christ as Paul did. They may be kind, loving people who appear to live almost as Christians, or on the other hand may be actively antagonistic towards God. But whether hostile, indifferent or interested, we long for something to happen that will cause them to come to know Christ for themselves. We do our best to pray for them, we try our best to talk to them, we set up opportunities for them to hear an explanation of the gospel, yet it all seems to no avail. The months pass into years and we see no progress or flicker of genuine spiritual understanding or receptivity to Christ. If only God would just strike them with a supernatural light from the sky, call them audibly by name, reveal himself irrefutably as Lord, and talk about a preordained plan for their lives, they would hardly have any choice but to respond and be converted.

But instead there is no light from heaven, no audible voice calling their name, no revealing of any plan for their lives, and they carry on as they always have, with little compelling reason to change.

God's initiative and human response

What actually happened on the road to Damascus? Is this supernatural intervention best explained as an arbitrary act of God, an expression of his sovereign irresistible election of an undeserving man to become his child, more dramatically expressed perhaps than the subtler inner witness of the Holy Spirit more commonly experienced by others? Some would say so, and with reason. Paul later writes to the Galatians about 'God who set me apart from birth and called me by his grace' (Galatians 1:15). They would believe Saul had been on God's hit list since birth (and before birth), and sovereignly choosing his moment, God caught him on the Damascus road and 'called [him] by his grace'.

It is unquestionably true that the initiative in the salvation of any human being belongs with God and not with us, for the Christian life does not begin with human discovery but with divine revelation. Paul himself writes, 'The man without the Spirit does not accept the things that come from the Spirit of God, for they are foolishness to him, and he cannot understand them, because they are spiritually discerned' (1 Corinthians 2:14) and also that 'no-one can say "Jesus is Lord," except by the Holy Spirit' (1 Corinthians 12:3). Jesus had taught that 'No-one can come to me unless the Father who sent me draws him' (John 6:44). From an open-minded reading of the Scriptures it is beyond question that God must initiate any saving knowledge we have of himself. What is equally true, however, is that this is not the sole ingredient in a person's salvation, nor, in this case, a complete explanation for Paul's dramatic conversion. A sovereign act of God is not the only part of the process that leads to salvation. While we must acknowledge that the initiative in revelation is, by definition, with the revealer, this is not purely an arbitrary act on God's part. We may also be confident, as the Scriptures teach, that humanity stands before God on level ground, and any person, from any background, with any history is a candidate for the revelation that comes from God. Paul writes of a general revelation that, if followed through, is sufficient to lead people to salvation, when he states, 'what may be known about God is plain to them, because God has made it plain to them', and then goes on to declare God's revelation of himself to a sufficient extent 'so that men are without excuse' (Romans 1:19–20).

If God has acted in revelation to place everyone beyond legitimate excuse, as Paul says, it is clearly insufficient to explain individual salvation solely in terms of the irresistible drawing power of God, for on those terms all would be saved, unless Paul is exaggerating the depth of revelation given to all people that leaves them 'without excuse'. There must be a reciprocating response to the revelation God gives, which is appropriated by some and not appropriated by others.

God's initiative is not to be questioned in the light of the fact that many people remain unsaved, despite his revelation. Jesus says to the people of Jerusalem:

> O Jerusalem, Jerusalem, you who kill the prophets and stone those sent to you, how often I have longed to gather your children together, as a hen gathers her chicks under her wings, but you were not willing. (Matthew 23:37)

Here we must either accept that the stumbling block to their being gathered to Christ was not the willingness of Jesus to gather them, but the unwillingness of the people to be gathered – or else we would have to conclude Jesus was weeping crocodile tears. Peter writes, 'He is patient with you, not wanting anyone to perish, but *everyone to come to repentance*' (2 Peter 3:9, my emphasis). If the willingness of Jesus is all it takes to secure a person's salvation, we should logically expect either some kind of universal salvation or hold God responsible for the dilemma of his wanting all to be saved, yet not providing the opportunity for that to take place. Both positions are in conflict with Scripture.

We must affirm that God alone saves, 'For it is by grace you have been saved, through faith – and this not from yourselves, it is the gift of God – not by works, so that no-one can boast' (Ephesians 2:8–9). But alongside that confidence in God's willingness and ability to save, it will also be helpful to us to investigate what we know of Paul at the time leading up to his conversion. The dramatic event outside the city of Damascus that changed Paul's life for ever, and through him profoundly influenced the world for the next two millennia, may not have taken place so completely 'out of the blue' as at first appears. Behind the antagonism and enmity towards Jesus Christ, effectively and dangerously displayed in Saul of Tarsus in his murderous exploits throughout Judea and its surrounding world, lay the very seeds of his own conversion. To construct a spiritual profile of Saul of Tarsus is to find all kinds of interweaving ingredients that contribute to the event which so forcibly and effectively changed his life – his encounter with the living Christ.

2

Profile of a Convert

There is always a reason why people behave as they do. Like the man found lying face down in the aisle of a cinema, who made no response when the usher and then the manager told him to get up and sit in a seat. When the police were eventually called and also failed to get his co-operation, they proceeded to arrest him, but first wanted to know where he had come from. For the first time he moved, looked up and said, 'The balcony.'

There was a reason why Paul behaved as he did. The roots that grow into the fruit of any conversion to Jesus Christ are put down long before a consciousness of saving grace is understood and experienced. Paul's encounter with Jesus on the Damascus road indicates much about his disposition of heart, in existence long before this encounter took place, and the seeds were actually sown in the unexpected ground of his opposition to Christ.

We are given sufficient detail of Paul's history prior to this event to enable us to establish something of a spiritual profile that may provide us with some vital clues as to his state of heart. Paul was born to Jewish parents in Tarsus, the capital of the Roman province of Cilicia (in modern-day Turkey), which he described as 'no ordinary city'. Although a Jew, Paul was born a Roman citizen (Acts 22:26–27), indicating his parents were already Roman citizens themselves. There is no indication of how his family obtained this distinction. Maybe his father or an earlier generation had rendered some outstanding service to Rome and had been rewarded with citizenship.

But Paul also describes himself as a 'Hebrew of Hebrews' (Philippians 3:5). His family could trace their descent from the tribe of Benjamin, and most likely gave their son his Jewish name, Saul, at the time of his circumcision when he was eight days old, in honour of the tribe's most illustrious member: the first king of Israel. His parents provided the best education available by sending him to Jerusalem to study under Gamaliel (see Acts 22:3). The little we know of Gamaliel reveals him as the outstanding and most prestigious teacher of his day. Gamaliel was given the title 'Rabban', higher than the more general 'Rabbi'. The Jewish Mishnah states, 'Since Rabban Gamaliel the Elder died there has been no more reverence for the law, and purity and abstinence died out at the same time.'[1] The only time Gamaliel makes an appearance in Scripture is as a member of the Sanhedrin Council in Jerusalem when they were discussing the suppression of Peter and the other apostles in the early days of the church. The majority wanted to put them to death, but Gamaliel intervened with the wise insight I referred to earlier:

> . . . I advise you: Leave these men alone! Let them go! For if their purpose or activity is of human origin, it will fail. But if it is from God, you will not be able to stop these men; you will only find yourselves fighting against God. (Acts 5:38–39)

This is not a foolproof criterion, for many things do exist and flourish that are self-evidently not of God. If Gamaliel

---

[1] See *New Bible Dictionary*, 'Gamaliel' (IVP, 1996).

remained true to his observation, perhaps in due course he too joined his pupil in becoming a disciple of Jesus Christ. There is no evidence, however, to suggest either way, other than the logic of his own stance.

Asking, seeking and knocking

We may be certain, though, that Gamaliel imparted to his pupil something of his love for the law of God, and would have encouraged this to become the prime motivating factor in Paul's life. When he explains to the Philippians the confidence of his pre-conversion days, Paul writes:

> If anyone else thinks he has reasons to put confidence in the flesh, I have more: circumcised on the eighth day, of the people of Israel, of the tribe of Benjamin, a Hebrew of Hebrews; in regard to the law, a Pharisee; as for zeal, persecuting the church; as for legalistic righteousness, faultless. (Philippians 3:4–6)

The zeal with which he persecuted the church derived from the zeal with which he held and kept the law of God. He stated in Jerusalem when arrested following his third missionary journey:

> Under Gamaliel I was thoroughly trained in the law of our fathers and was just as zealous for God as any of you are today. I persecuted the followers of this Way to their death, arresting both men and women and throwing them into prison . . . (Acts 22:3–4)

As an utterly committed Jew, zealous for God, he reasoned this way: If Judaism is truth, anything that detracts from or contradicts its doctrines and practices is by definition untrue and therefore false. Consequently, any movement threatening Judaism must be opposed and stopped. If the only effective way to destroy such a movement was to imprison its leaders and threaten them with murder, then imprison and murder them he would. Such was Paul's commitment and the logic of his actions against the church. It was not primarily a negative anger at the early Christians that motivated Saul, but a positive and rigorous defence of the law he loved and believed was being undermined by them. In his anger and persecution of the church he was trying to please God in the only way he knew how; he believed his opposition to this new movement was with God's approval and could be carried out with his blessing!

In all probability, the apostles in Jerusalem did not know this. They were fully aware of Paul's existence, but knew him only as an enemy. When he was brought back to Jerusalem some time after his conversion they where highly sceptical: 'they were all afraid of him, not believing that he really was a disciple' (Acts 9:26). They assumed the story of his conversion to be a clever tactic to infiltrate their movement, so as to enable him to better identify their leaders, root out their followers and destroy their strategies. They did not know that the motivation behind his earlier antagonism towards them had been birthed in a fear of God and a desire to do his will. They could only see the outward expression of his enmity towards them. As God had said to Samuel about David so many years before, 'The LORD does not look at the things man looks at. Man looks at the outward appearance, but the LORD looks at the heart' (1 Samuel 16:7). The apostles and disciples in Jerusalem looked on the outward appearance of Saul and saw an enemy of God. God looked on his heart and saw a man trying with all his might to please him.

It is the disposition of a person's heart, in conjunction with the revealing work of the Holy Spirit, that opens a person to the grace of God. Jesus said:

Ask and it will be given to you; seek and you will find; knock and the door will be opened to you. For everyone who asks receives; he who seeks finds; and to him who knocks, the door will be opened. (Matthew 7:7–8)

If someone may legitimately claim, 'I want to find God but can't,' then this statement of Jesus is an exaggeration. The ones who do not find God, says Jesus, are the ones who do not seek God, for 'he who seeks finds'. Those who do not receive are those who do not ask, for 'everyone who asks receives'. Those to whom the door remains closed are those who do not knock, for 'to him who knocks, the door will be opened'. It is to everyone who asks, seeks and knocks that the promise of finding, receiving and the door opening is made.

What then, we may ask, happens to people who ask for the wrong thing, who seek in the wrong direction or who knock on the wrong door? God in his mercy and kindness gives them the right thing, takes them in the right direction and opens to them the right door. Saul of Tarsus was knocking loudly on the wrong door. He sought righteousness through his own disciplined keeping of the law, and to some extent deceived himself into thinking he was successful, claiming to have been 'as for legalistic righteousness, faultless' (Philippians 3:6). He did not know prior to his Damascus road experience that the only legitimate righteousness was that which derived from God and not from his own disciplined self-effort. His discovery of this fact, in due course, became the main thrust of his writing and ministry, but his initial pursuit of righteousness by human discipline and obedience masked not a pursuit of self-interest and fulfilment for his own ends, but a genuine desire to please God. As a man who was seeking so conscientiously and knocking so relentlessly, he was destined to find what he was looking for, and the right door would one day swing open.

Seeking souls always find

Saul of Tarsus was not unique in this. In the first twelve chapters of Acts (prior to Paul's first missionary journey) there are
only three stories of individual conversions: the Ethiopian
eunuch (chapter 8), Saul of Tarsus (chapter 9) and Cornelius
the Roman centurion (chapter 10). A pattern of asking, seeking
and knocking can be discerned in each case, long before their
coming into an encounter with the living Christ.

What had the Ethiopian eunuch been doing in Jerusalem
when Philip met him on his homeward journey? Acts records,
'This man had gone to Jerusalem to worship' (Acts 8:27). There
had been a considerable impact made on the Ethiopians by
Jewish life and thought and, like a number of his countrymen,
this high official, treasurer in the court of the Ethiopian Queen
Candace, was almost certainly a proselyte to Judaism. If not,
he was evidently seeking to find God through the rituals and
practices of Judaism, particularly through its temple activity.
This accounts for the long trek he had made from his own
country to Jerusalem. Returning home disillusioned, he was in
his chariot reading the words of Isaiah the prophet from an
open scroll in his hand, but was unable to make sense of its
meaning. At that moment, with his enquiring but confused
mind contemplating the open scroll in front of him, Philip
joined him in the chariot, explained the passage, and led him to
Christ. The Ethiopian had been asking, seeking and knocking
in the best way he knew. He was almost knocking on the right
door, but not quite, and disillusioned with the apparent lack of
satisfaction from his visit to Jerusalem was returning home
deeply disappointed, for he was leaving as empty as he had
arrived. Knowing the disposition of his heart, God sent Philip
to the desert road to open the right door for him and bring him
to Christ. Long before the Ethiopian's conversion on the desert

road, a hunger to find God had already been awakened in his heart.

The conversion of Saul of Tarsus is recorded next (in Acts 9), and then that of Cornelius in Caesarea (see Acts 10). Cornelius was a good man, an officer of the occupying Roman army. He gave generously to the poor, had built a synagogue for the Jews, and was evidently a man of prayer. Yet none of his goodness, generous giving or fervent prayers made him a Christian. They were merely positive features of his life affirmed by the angel who appeared to him in a vision and said, 'Your prayers and gifts to the poor have come up as a memorial offering before God' (Acts 10:4). Although his good works were completely inadequate to save him, God recognized and was pleased with the disposition of heart that lay behind them. These good works had come before the Lord as 'a memorial offering'. Cornelius had been genuinely seeking – but in the wrong direction. He had been sincerely knocking – but on the wrong door. It was this disposition of heart towards God that made him ripe for the revelation of Christ and the encounter with his Spirit that came when God sent the apostle Peter to his door to point him to Christ.

We can go back to the first record of anyone in the New Testament being described as worshipping Jesus – the Magi who came from the east 'to worship him' (Matthew 2:2). These men were not necessarily people of great conventional wisdom, but as the term 'Magi' implies, they practised magical arts and astrology. There has been much speculation as to the actual star, or combination of stars, the Magi saw, but it was evidently their profession to watch the night skies, where at one time they saw what spoke to them of the entry of a king into the world. Possibly this was something entirely unique and miraculous that cannot be explained naturally (like the visit of the angels to the shepherds), but it is more likely to have been a natural phenomenon, which had caused these men to ponder its meaning and set out to follow its message.[2] Foretelling the future from the stars was a common practice in those days (as is the widespread use of astrology in our day), and any interruption to the normal orderly routine of the heavens was given particular interpretation.

We cannot know for sure, but it is interesting, if not extraordinary, to observe that reading the stars brought these particular men to Christ. Astrology in the Bible is mentioned with scorn and rebuke for any dependency placed on it.[3] There may be knowledge obtainable through astrology – but it is forbidden knowledge, and is unrelated to divine revelation. It is remarkable, therefore, that these Magi, engaging in reading the stars, should be brought by that understanding to Christ. It was not astrology that brought them to Christ, but the disposition of their hearts that expressed their genuine seeking of God, and their willingness to knock on any door that might bring them in touch with God. In their case, this subsequently brought them on a mission to Bethlehem and enabled them to find the truth. This is not to suggest for one moment that anyone involved in astrology, or any other religious activity, or who is dabbling with other forms of twenty-first century spirituality, is by definition seeking God, for clearly that is not true. Most religious activity today seems to be driven by the creed of self-fulfilment, not a hunger for God. Many people are merely responding to their own superstitions, some escaping the less palatable realities of life with which they struggle to cope, and others looking for an alternative to the materialism that leaves them so empty, none of which involves a genuine seeking for God. For a few, of course, there is money

---

[2] See Charles Price, *Matthew* (Christian Focus Publications, 1998), pp. 26ff.

[3] See, for example, Isaiah 47:13–14.

to be made in exploiting vulnerable people who are willing to believe some of the nonsense they are told about spirituality. As G.K. Chesterton famously stated, 'When people stop believing in God, they don't believe in nothing, they believe in anything,' and our post-Christian era demonstrates loudly the truth of that insight.

It remains true, however, that when people genuinely seek for God, they will find him, for Jesus promised it. We will therefore know true seekers by the fact that in due course they find him. The genuineness of the Magi is evident in that when they came to Jesus, they recognized him 'and worshipped him. Then they opened their treasures' (Matthew 2:11). True seeking of God is not marked by a primary wish to gain, but to give in worship to him, expressed by the Magi in 'opening their treasures' and giving that which was costly.

It is not God's unwillingness to be 'found' that is the reason for our ignorance of him, but our unwillingness to 'seek'. Furthermore, we may say that every one of us who has come to know God in some measure, goes on to know as much of him as he or she sincerely wants to know. God told Israel in Moses' day as they prepared to enter Canaan for the first time that one day in their future they would be driven out of the land and go into exile, but that 'if from there you seek the LORD your God, you will find him if you look for him with all your heart and with all your soul' (Deuteronomy 4:29). The same promise was repeated to Jeremiah when centuries later they found themselves driven into exile: 'You will seek me and find me when you seek me with all your heart' (Jeremiah 29:13). Finding God is not only possible to those who seek him, but it is promised!

What awakens the desire to seek for God in the first place is an important point to consider but is not the issue at this stage, except to acknowledge that Paul writes regarding our natural disposition, 'there is . . . no-one who seeks God' (Romans 3:11), and it takes the Holy Spirit to awaken that desire. Our concern, however, is to recognize that the dramatic conversion of Saul of Tarsus on the road to Damascus was not a coincidental event, but a logical and inevitable consequence of the attitude of heart that underlay his activities – he wanted to know and please God and was therefore destined in the course of time to do so. His discovery of God in the person of Jesus Christ, despite his active opposition to Christ, was in reality a conversion waiting to happen. It was only a matter of time before the God he actively opposed while attempting to please, would lift the veil of Paul's heart and bring him into an encounter with his Son.

In the family

There is, however, perhaps even more than immediately meets the eye in the events surrounding Paul's conversion, as is true in most cases. Not only was Paul's antagonism to the early church a symptom of his desire to serve and please God, but through his writings we discover that among the first believers were members of Paul's own family. He writes to the church in Rome, 'Greet Andronicus and Junias, my relatives who have been in prison with me. They are outstanding among the apostles, and they were in Christ before I was' (Romans 16:7). This intriguing reference to relatives (perhaps husband and wife) gives us no detail as to their exact relationship to Paul, where and when they were imprisoned with him, how and when they themselves had become believers (other than that their conversion preceded Paul's), or why they were resident in Rome at the time Paul wrote to the Romans. In fact, there were four other believing relatives of Paul in Rome to whom he made reference, making six in all. The others are named as Herodion, Lucius, Jason and Sosipater to whom he makes just one reference each in the same letter (Romans 16:11, 21).

To have been 'in Christ before I was' indicates their conversions to have been very early on in the church's story, and the comment 'They are outstanding among the apostles' suggests they either were well known in Jerusalem, or perhaps were themselves recognized as 'apostles'. Various possible suggestions about them have been made, such as that they were among those described as 'visitors from Rome' who heard Peter preach on the Day of Pentecost and were of the three thousand who were converted that day (see Acts 2:10). Perhaps they were also among the five hundred who saw the Lord after his resurrection (see 1 Corinthians 15:6). Whatever the truth, the intriguing thing is that Paul had relatives who were Christians before he was. No doubt, at the very least they were praying for him, for it was their relative Paul who was a prime enemy of the new church of which they were a part. How much, we may wonder, did their prayer and involvement in Paul's life contribute to the events surrounding his conversion?

All in all, there are eight relatives of Paul mentioned in the New Testament, the six we have already mentioned living in Rome, but an even closer family connection is found in a reference to Paul's sister and nephew (Acts 23:16) who lived in Jerusalem at the time of his arrest after his third missionary journey. His sister heard of the plot of over 40 Jewish men to fast until they had killed Paul, and sent her son to inform Paul of this in the barracks where he was being held. He had his nephew taken to the commander who on hearing of the plot ordered Paul's removal to Caesarea as a precaution. This is again a tantalizingly brief reference to relatives of Paul. Was his sister a Christian? She was certainly sympathetic to his situation. If she was a Christian, when did she become one? Was it before Paul, similar to their relatives Andronicus and Junias, or was it afterwards, perhaps as a result of Paul's own conversion? We do not have the answers to those questions, but it is interesting to know that in the background of Paul's life are family members who may also have played some role, perhaps by their prayers, in contributing to his conversion on the Damascus road.

Discovering Jesus Christ is alive

The decisive issue that precipitated Paul's change of heart was the discovery that Jesus Christ was alive. He did not meet a representative of Christ on the Damascus road, nor experience an apparition, for the sound of Christ's voice was heard by Paul's companions, though they did not understand the words. This was an encounter with the living Christ himself. In genuine Christianity this remains the pivotal issue. Until the discovery is made that Jesus Christ is actually alive, Christianity can and will never make sense. Christianity is so much more than implementing the teaching of the historical Christ, or modelling his example, or adopting his lifestyle. The fact of the resurrection of Jesus Christ from the dead, and the implications of his being alive are central to Paul's gospel to the extent that he states there is no gospel without the risen Christ: 'And if Christ has not been raised, our preaching is useless and so is your faith . . . And if Christ has not been raised, your faith is futile; you are still in your sins' (1 Corinthians 15:14, 17). This is evident too in the 40 days Jesus spent with his disciples following his resurrection and prior to his ascension when 'he showed himself to these men and gave many convincing proofs that he was alive' (Acts 1:3). It seems perhaps strange that 'many convincing proofs' were necessary. One should be sufficient evidence that someone is alive! Clearly it was indispensable to the experience and message of these disciples that the one non-negotiable issue was not just the fact that Jesus *was* raised from the dead as a historical event, but that he *is* alive as a present ongoing reality.

Christ being alive has to Paul both an objective and a subjective aspect. Objectively he summarizes the irreducible content of the gospel to 'Christ died for our sins according to the Scriptures, that he was buried, that he was raised on the third day according to the Scriptures' (1 Corinthians 15:3ff.) and then goes to lengths in giving a list of the people to whom he appeared after his resurrection and who were physical eyewitnesses to this fact. He claims this witness for himself, 'Have I not seen Jesus our Lord?' (1 Corinthians 9:1), which may be a direct reference to his encounter with Christ on the road to Damascus.

However, the objective truth of the resurrection of Christ must also become a reality in subjective experience. Writing to the Galatians Paul says, 'But when God, who set me apart from birth and called me by his grace, was pleased to *reveal his Son in me* so that I might preach him among the Gentiles' (Galatians 1:15–16, my emphasis). He is saying that the revelation of the risen Christ *to* him became the revelation of the risen Christ *in* him. Having been raised from the dead historically, his purpose is to impart his resurrected life to the believer experientially. Paul writes of 'Christ, who *is* your life' (Colossians 3:4, my emphasis). He is not only the giver of life, but the life itself! He writes of 'Christ in you, the hope of glory' (Colossians 1:27); 'I no longer live, but Christ lives in me' (Galatians 2:20); 'For we who are alive are always being given over to death for Jesus' sake, so that *his life* may be revealed in our mortal body' (2 Corinthians 4:11, my emphasis). This is Paul speaking of the fact that spiritual life is the risen life of Christ imparted to the Christian by the Holy Spirit. The reception of this life constitutes regeneration. It is therefore logical that Paul's acid test of Christian experience is the evidence of the indwelling presence of Jesus Christ in the Christian. He asked the Corinthians to 'Examine yourselves to see whether you are in the faith; test yourselves. Do you not realize that Christ Jesus is in you – unless, of course, you fail the test?' (2 Corinthians 13:5). The union of a Christian with Christ, where the believer receives the actual life of Christ, is central to Paul's writings and preaching, the implications of which we will explore more fully later on.

Revelation leads to regeneration

Although Saul of Tarsus met Jesus on the Damascus road, he did not in truth become a Christian at that point. The definition Paul gives of a Christian is one in whom lives the Spirit of Christ, 'And if anyone does not have the Spirit of Christ, he does not belong to Christ' (Romans 8:9b). The immediate consequence of Paul's encounter on the Damascus road was not regeneration (the receiving of new life) but revelation (the receiving of new understanding). The immediate result was a state of physical blindness that lasted three days, during which time his companions took him into Damascus to the home of a man named Judas who lived on Straight Street. The blindness symbolized the darkness of his own soul in the natural state of separation from God that is true of all people. When Paul was in Damascus, God spoke to a disciple named Ananias and sent him to the home where Saul was staying. Meanwhile, Saul in prayer had experienced a vision of Ananias coming to place his hands on him in order that the work that had begun on the Damascus road might be completed.

After three days of being in Damascus, Ananias came to Paul and two things took place, both of which constitute the ingredients necessary to spiritual new birth: his sins were forgiven and he received the gift of the Holy Spirit. In Paul's own testimony about the event, given many years later before a crowd in Jerusalem, he recalled Ananias saying to him, 'And now what are you waiting for? Get up, be baptised and wash your sins away, calling on his name' (Acts 22:16). Evidently, despite his encounter with Christ three days earlier, his sins had not yet been washed away, an event symbolized in the washing of baptism. Luke also records that Ananias then placed his hands on Saul and said to him, 'Brother Saul, the Lord – Jesus, who appeared to you on the road as you were coming here – has sent me so that you may see again and be filled with the Holy Spirit' (Acts 9:17). The dual activity of forgiveness and washing away of sin and receiving the Holy Spirit are the essential ingredients in true conversion. Saul came under conviction of his need on the Damascus road, symbolized in the three days of blindness that followed, but he was born again when Ananias visited him three days later. Having been forgiven of sin which separates us from God, it is the gift of the Holy Spirit that brings us into union with Christ, and the relationship whereby he lives in us and we in him.

Further to his discovery that Jesus Christ was alive, Paul recognized immediately the implications of this by addressing him as Lord: 'Who are you, Lord?' (Acts 9:5). From that day on he had no plans of his own, for there was now a new master of his life, and his responsibilities were to be found in an unquestioning obedience to Christ for the fulfilment of his plans through Paul. The rest of Paul's life is explicable only in these terms. In nearly all 13 of Paul's letters in the New Testament he introduces himself in terms of his service to Jesus Christ: 'Paul, a servant of Christ Jesus' (Romans 1:1); 'called to be an apostle of Christ Jesus by the will of God' (1 Corinthians 1:1); 'an apostle – sent not from men nor by man, but by Jesus Christ' (Galatians 1:1); 'a servant of God' (Titus 1:1); 'a prisoner of Christ Jesus' (Philemon 1). The only two letters in which he does not introduce himself in this way are the two letters to the Thessalonians, but the same issue is fundamental in his message in those letters too, summarized in his statement 'we instructed you how to live in order to please God' (1 Thessalonians 4:1). The life of Saul of Tarsus following his meeting with Jesus is explicable only in terms of the lordship of Christ over him governing his direction, and the Spirit of Christ within him, giving him the dynamic resources necessary to fulfil the will of God.

It is difficult to establish a precise chronology of Paul's' life, but it was at least 12 or possibly 14 years after his conversion before he travelled on his first missionary journey and engaged in the ministry to the Gentile world for which he is best known. How did God prepare him during those years? How does the will of God become worked out in daily experience and in our own lives? It is to that we must now turn.

3

Motivated by Vision

What happened during those intervening years between Paul's conversion and his first missionary journey? In an attempt to reconstruct this period, several events come to light that have considerable bearing on the years that followed. These represent key events that not only contributed significantly to equipping Paul for his ministry, but are universally relevant issues in equipping all of God's people for the fulfilment of whatever his particular plan for their lives may be.

The first and possibly most significant is what Paul himself described as 'a vision from heaven'. A quarter of a century after his conversion, Paul spent two years imprisoned in Caesarea, where the governor Felix kept him in prison to maintain his own popularity with the Jews in Jerusalem, while at the same time being willing to be bribed to set him free. Paul did not pay bribes so he endured two solitary years in the Caesarean jail until Felix was recalled to Rome and replaced by Porcius Festus. One of Festus' first visitors was King Agrippa, grandson of the notorious 'Herod the tetrarch', who had executed John the Baptist and who came to Caesarea to pay his respects to the new Roman governor. Festus discussed Paul's case with the king, and Agrippa requested that he meet Paul for himself.

When he did so, Paul gave his account of meeting the risen
Christ on the Damascus road and some detail of the conversa-
tion between them both:

> Then I asked, 'Who are you, Lord?'
>
> 'I am Jesus, whom you are persecuting,' the Lord replied. 'Now
> get up and stand on your feet. I have appeared to you to appoint
> you as a servant and as a witness of what you have seen of me and
> what I will show you. I will rescue you from your own people and
> from the Gentiles. I am sending you to them to open their eyes and
> turn them from darkness to light, and from the power of Satan to
> God, so that they may receive forgiveness of sins and a place among
> those who are sanctified by faith in me.'
>
> So then, King Agrippa, I was not disobedient to the vision from
> heaven. First to those in Damascus, then to those in Jerusalem and
> in all Judea, and to the Gentiles also, I preached that they should
> repent and turn to God and prove their repentance by their deeds.
> (Acts 26:15–20)

Paul affirms that for 25 years he has been obedient to 'the
vision from heaven', something God first gave him in embryo
form on the Damascus road, and which was fleshed out a little
by Ananias when he came to him in Damascus a few days later,
and brought to fruition through the long years of apostleship.
That sense of vision was a key factor in motivating and sustaining Paul during the silent years before his first missionary
travels, and in the many dark and difficult experiences that followed.

If this was true for Paul, I suggest that a sense of vision
should be an equally sustaining feature in our lives too. By
'vision' I don't mean something that comes in the night after
eating too much strong cheese, but a clear and progressive sense
of direction, which has its origin in God. Solomon writes,
'Where there is no vision, the people perish' (Proverbs 29:18,

AV). That is to say, without vision people live sloppily, dry up, lose their way and are destroyed.

Not only during the long period before his first missionary journey did Paul's vision sustain him, but continually through the years of his missionary enterprise, characterized almost relentlessly by a series of conflicts, troubles, setbacks and imprisonments. Yet he kept in focus what God had shown him in the early days. Now, standing before King Agrippa, already deprived of a two-year period of freedom by the corrupt Roman judicial system, he was neither crushed nor despondent about events, for he could say, 'I was not disobedient to the vision from heaven.' In pursuit of the vision he received from God, the details of what happened to him in the process were almost an irrelevance, for he was on divine business, fulfilling a divine call, depending on divine resources!

The cause of Paul's circumstances was more important to him than the circumstances themselves. He said of his Roman imprisonment, when writing to the Philippians, 'I am put here for the defence of the gospel' (Philippians 1:16). There was no need for panic or desperation in appalling circumstances. It was God who had put him there. Chained to Roman guards in a place he would not have chosen to be, Paul was not now exempt from his ministry; rather, he simply had another opportunity to fulfil it, so that

> what has happened to me has really served to advance the gospel. As a result, it has become clear throughout the whole palace guard and to everyone else that I am in chains for Christ. (Philippians 1:12–13)

He concludes his letter to the Philippians by saying, 'All the saints send you greetings, especially those who belong to Caesar's household.' Why were there saints in Caesar's household? The reason was because Paul was in Caesar's prison, and his mandate to preach the gospel did not cease because of the corruption of the legal system that had failed to free him as it should have done. On the contrary, he was still carrying out his original brief.

Beginning with the end in mind

In his best-selling book on self-management, *The Seven Habits of Highly Effective People*[1], Stephen Covey puts as a top priority the need to 'begin with the end in mind'. He makes the statement 'All things are created twice. There's a mental or first creation and a physical or second creation to all things.' Before anything successful is accomplished there must be a clear vision of the end product. Before a builder digs the first piece of ground for the foundation he has a blueprint showing what the building is going to be.

The apostle Paul did not become an apostle to the Gentile world by accident! He wasn't looking for some kind of job in the Christian ministry, vaguely searching around for something he thought might be suitable, slowly working his way up the ranks until he found to his astonishment he was evangelizing the Gentile world! He was fulfilling a mandate he had been given by God, and only sought to obey the vision from heaven. Nothing else was really at stake.

We can reconstruct the means by which Paul received this vision from various accounts in the book of Acts, some of which he himself gave. In his account to Agrippa he records that his vocation, as told him by the Lord Jesus on the Damascus road, was essentially that of a preacher of the gospel to both Jews and Gentiles, for the purpose of bringing about

---

[1] Stephen Covey, *The Seven Habits of Highly Effective People* (Simon and Schuster, 1994).

their forgiveness and sanctification through dependency on Jesus Christ. In his account to the crowd in Jerusalem, following his arrest prior to his imprisonment in Caesarea, he told them that Ananias had said to him, 'You will be his witness to all men of what you have seen and heard' (Acts 22:15). Luke in his account of Paul's conversion tells us that the Lord had told Ananias, 'This man is my chosen instrument to carry my name before the Gentiles and their kings and before the people of Israel. I will show him how much he must suffer for my name' (Acts 9:15). Jesus' own words to Paul on the Damascus road had hinted at this suffering aspect: 'I will rescue you from your own people and from the Gentiles.' We therefore know that the day Paul was converted to Jesus Christ, he knew something of his destiny. He would preach the gospel to Jew and Gentile in the face of opposition and suffering.

Paul's claim to King Agrippa that 'I was not disobedient to the vision from heaven' put him into a long line of men and women who began with the end in mind. They had listened as God revealed his plan and purpose and lived with this insight tucked away in the back of their minds, pursuing God's vision and awaiting his timing for it to be fully brought to fruition. This is not intended to be a characteristic unique to a few aristocrats of Scripture, but part of the ministry of the Holy Spirit in the lives of his ordinary regenerate people. Peter explained the significance of Pentecost by quoting the prophet Joel:

> In the last days, God says,
> I will pour out my Spirit on all people.
> Your sons and daughters will prophesy,
> your young men will see visions,
> your old men will dream dreams. (Acts 2:17)

Seeing visions and dreaming dreams is to be part of the era of the Holy Spirit indwelling his people. This was not something

altogether new at Pentecost, but like the availability of the Holy
Spirit, was universalized at Pentecost and made available to all
God's people.

David had written a thousand years before:

> Delight yourself in the LORD
> and he will give you the desires of your heart. (Psalm 37:4)

This does not refer to the desires of our hearts being met, but
the desires themselves being implanted in our hearts by the
Lord in the first place. As we 'delight ourselves in the Lord' his
interests become our interests and his desires become our
desires. Paul writes, 'For it is God who works in you to will and
to act according to his good purpose' (Philippians 2:13). The
very desire, the 'will', is God given.

When we ask God to show us his will, we often want him to
give us a road map, whereas what he is more likely to give us is
a compass. We do not need to know the twists and turns along
the way, but we do need to know the direction. Paul's statement
to King Agrippa 'I was not disobedient to the vision from
heaven' does not refer to any advanced knowledge of the details
of his life, but to the compass bearing that was set by the Lord
Jesus Christ for Paul on the road to Damascus, and which ever
since had been the governing principle of his vocation. Hence
when he writes to the Romans, he justifies his desire to go to
Rome by saying, 'I am bound both to Greeks and non-Greeks,
both to the wise and the foolish. That is why I am so eager to
preach the gospel also to you who are at Rome' (Romans
1:14–15). Paul was not motivated by a desire to travel, or an
ambition to establish a network of churches over which he
could preside. His obligation derived from his vision expressed
in his sense of purpose and destiny! He was not a driven man
so much as a drawn man, drawn by the power of a God-given

vision, which he had seen and which he gave his energies to fulfil. In his last letter, written to Timothy in the concluding years of his life, he writes:

> For I am already being poured out like a drink offering, and the time has come for my departure. I have fought the good fight, I have finished the race, I have kept the faith. Now there is in store for me the crown of righteousness, which the Lord, the righteous Judge, will award to me on that day . . . (2 Timothy 4:6–8)

The journey had been long and lonely, the road had been steep and hard, but he had only run on the road Jesus Christ had set him on, and he was satisfied.

This clear vision of what his future would consist of is not unique in Scripture to Paul. Many leading characters in the Bible were similarly characterized by vision – they were able to start with the end in mind, and know a much deeper significance to their lives and activities than was obvious to anyone else.

People of vision

Abraham

God showed Abraham the stars of the night sky and told him that his descendants would be as numerous as them, despite the fact that he was already 75, his wife Sarah was 65 and they had been unable to conceive children throughout the long years of their marriage. However, it was another 25 years before God gave them the son he had promised. During those years, Abraham lived with only a sense that God had spoken and that one day his promise would come to pass. He lived with vision.

Hagar

Hagar became the mother of Abraham's first son, Ishmael, conceived after the suggestion of Abraham's wife Sarah, when her apparent infertility seemed to render impossible God's promise of a son. This form of surrogate motherhood, where a servant would bear a child for her mistress, was not abnormal in the culture of their day. The pregnancy created such jealousy on the part of Sarah that she mistreated Hagar, causing her to flee the household. While sitting near a spring in the desert, the angel of the Lord (God incarnate in angelic form[2]), appeared to her asking the question 'Hagar, servant of Sarai, where have you come from, and where are you going?' (Genesis 16:8). He then made a promise concerning her unborn son: 'I will so increase your descendants that they will be too numerous to count.'

Thirteen years after the birth of Ishmael, Sarah gave birth to Abraham's promised son Isaac. When Isaac was weaned, Ishmael mocked him, causing Sarah to have Hagar and Ishmael dismissed from the household, so as to deprive them of any share in Abraham's inheritance. They wandered in the desert to Beersheba, and having exhausted their few provisions, Hagar put Ishmael under a bush to die, as she sat nearby sobbing. At this point the angel of God appeared again, saying, 'Do not be afraid . . . Lift the boy up and take him by the hand, for I will make him into a great nation' (Genesis 21:17–18). Hagar was again given a vision by God for the future of her rejected son, a vision that in her despair of their current circumstances she was forgetting. She was told the second time that Ishmael would have many descendants (whom we know now as the Arab race), and that God would make them a great nation. It is true, as the angel told Hagar:

---

[2] Occurrences of 'The angel of the Lord' are preincarnate appearances of Christ, known as either a *Christophany* or a *theophany*. This is evident in the appearance to Hagar for she addresses him, 'You are the God who sees me . . . I have now seen the One who sees me' (Genesis 16:13).

He will be a wild donkey of a man;
>   his hand will be against everyone
>   and everyone's hand against him,
and he will live in hostility
>   towards all his brothers. (Genesis 16:12)

But through it all God would carve a destiny that would make
Ishmael's descendants a great people. Hagar saw it in advance.
She lived with vision.

Joseph, son of Jacob

At the age of 17, Joseph dreamed of his brothers bowing to
him. His brothers hated him for his precocious behaviour, and
in jealousy got rid of him, selling him as a slave to the
Midianites. The highest bidder in the Egyptian slave market,
Potiphar, purchased him and took him to work in his home. He
quickly became impressed with Joseph's character and integrity
and put him in charge of his household. Potiphar's wife was
also impressed with this handsome young man and tried to
seduce him. He fled and she accused him of attempting to rape
her. Potiphar, believing his wife, had Joseph thrown into prison
where he remained forgotten for years until he interpreted the
king's dream about seven lean cows eating seven fat cows and
remaining lean. By this time he was 30 years old, 13 years after
being sold on the slave market. He warned Pharaoh that a
seven-year period of plenty would be followed by a seven-year
period of famine, and all preparations should be made during
the time of plenty for the coming famine. Joseph was himself
appointed to plan and execute the survival programme.

Two years into the famine (Joseph was now 39 years of age)
his brothers came from Canaan to buy food to alleviate the
famine they too were experiencing. The brothers were brought
in before Joseph and 'they bowed down to him with their faces

to the ground' (Genesis 42:6). Joseph recognized them, and then 'he remembered his dreams about them' (verse 9). For 22 years Joseph had been the slave of Potiphar, then a prisoner of a miscarriage of justice, and finally a key minister in the Egyptian government, second only to Pharaoh himself, but through all that time there was in the back of his mind a dream . . . a vision. God had shown him something and it would come to pass. How it would work out he could not have been able to forecast, but a day would come when his brothers would bow down to him. Many years after they had sold him as a slave and thought they would never see him again, the day came, and they bowed before him exactly as Joseph had seen them doing in his dream.

Moses

At the age of 40, Moses had a sense of destiny. Born to Hebrew parents but by 'chance' reared as a prince in Egypt, he had a clear sense of vision, and expected others to share it: 'Moses thought that his own people would realize that God was using him to rescue them, but they did not' (Acts 7:25). Why Moses believed this we are not told, but somehow he had found this sense of destiny. At 40 he blew it by killing an Egyptian and then fleeing to the Midian desert for his own safety. Another 40 years would pass before God met him as a man of 80 at the burning bush and told him, 'I am sending you to Pharaoh to bring my people the Israelites out of Egypt' (Exodus 3:10). During those long years of exile he may well have remembered the vision that had motivated him at 40, and waited for God's timing.

David

God sent the prophet Samuel to the home of Jesse in Bethlehem to find a replacement king for Saul, long before David was able to accede to the throne. God put the crown on David's head as a teenage boy many years before the elders crowned him in Hebron at the age of 30. David had opportunities to kill Saul and speed his path to the throne, but refused to do so. He knew his destiny and that it was God's prerogative to fulfil it without any manipulation of events by David. He lived many difficult years as a fugitive on the run from Saul, but with a sense of vision that one day his destiny would be realized.

If we look at people like Ezra and Nehemiah, at some of the good kings of Judah, and prophets like Isaiah and Jeremiah we will find this characteristic in common: they began with the end in mind, and that end was given them by God. They knew they were going somewhere and despite the obstacles and frustrations could see around the corners and over the horizon. They were men of vision.

Joseph, Jesus' earthly father

In the New Testament, Joseph was told by an angel that Mary was pregnant with a baby conceived by the Holy Spirit, and 'to give him the name Jesus, because he will save his people from their sins' (Matthew 1:21). Joseph never lived to see that fulfilled, as it seems that he died sometime after Jesus reached maturity at the age of twelve, where Joseph makes his last appearance in the Scriptures. He lived through all the trauma and criticisms of having a child born out of wedlock, but every time he tucked his little boy into bed he knew the boy had a destiny. He was a man with vision. Mary herself saw the future with both its glory and its pain. She was told, 'And a sword will pierce your own soul too' (Luke 2:35). As one of those at the foot of the cross when her son was put to death, she was not taken by surprise. She had known for more than 30 years that the sword was coming, and hidden the truths in her heart waiting for their fulfilment. Jesus himself at the age of twelve declared that he was 'about my Father's business' (Luke 2:49

AV). It would be another 18 years before his Father would set him apart at his baptism for public ministry.

Finding a vision

To illustrate this principle, let me share something from my own experience. At the age of 16 I knew God was calling me to preach. I didn't tell anyone, nor did it seem to me a natural thing for me to do. I plucked up courage at the age of 17 to tell an evangelist friend of mine while sitting in his car in the dark (the darkness gave me courage, for I felt acutely embarrassed by my presumption). His advice was not what I expected, but it was tremendously helpful. He told me not to go into Christian ministry if I could possibly do anything else and still be happy. (I later discovered that was the advice that the famous nineteenth-century preacher, C.H. Spurgeon, gave his students.) Confirmation that I could not do anything else and be happy came one day when I stumbled across the statement of Jeremiah:

> But if I say, 'I will not mention him
>   or speak any more in his name,'
> his word is in my heart like a fire,
>   a fire shut up in my bones.
> I am weary of holding it in;
>   indeed, I cannot. (Jeremiah 20:9)

I knew when I read it that that was how I felt.

In the course of time I graduated from a Bible college in Glasgow with a clear general sense of direction that my calling was to preach, but I had no specific way forward. For that first summer I had sufficient invitations to lead camps and youth missions around the country so that for the first three months my time was full and the pressure was off to sort out anything for the long term. When autumn came, the next three months had also filled, and included in the various invitations that came my way were offers of full-time employment with several evangelistic or youth organizations. In fact, by December that year I had six firm invitations to consider, including opportunities for employment as an evangelist, or in church pastoral ministry or a mixture of administration and preaching. I didn't know which of the six would be right, so went to seek the advice of a wise Christian man. I explained my dilemma and he told me he couldn't help me decide which of the six might be right because I obviously didn't have a clear vision of the direction God wanted me to go in the first place – only a vague sense I should preach. I didn't consider this the most helpful advice I had ever received! He went on to talk about asking God for a clear vision. He was the first (and only) person to talk to me about having a vision from God and I shall be for ever grateful to him.

Soon after that meeting, I went away for two days with just my Bible, a notebook and a pen. During those two days I asked God to give me a clear sense of direction for the future and a vision that would set the compass of my life. I had no idea of how to go about that, so on the basis of the statement 'He will give you the desires of your heart' I began to write down what I would really like to do if it were entirely up to me, trusting that perhaps what I really wanted was also what God wanted. At the end of those two days, which included a lot of walking, thinking, praying and reading my Bible, I had a list of six things I believed would determine my future. I then took these six pointers back to the six invitations awaiting a reply from me and found that they did not match with one of them. It was a difficult day when I wrote to all six, thanking them for their invitation but saying I did not think this was the right thing for me to do. When I mailed the letters I felt both a disappointment (I had no alternative avenue open to me) and at the same time a tremendous sense of exhilaration that I was free to do only what God wanted.

Less than a week later I found myself making an unplanned visit to Capernwray Hall in the north of England. The founder and then director of Capernwray, Major Ian Thomas, who spent most of his time travelling the world, happened to be home. He invited me for a cup of coffee and asked what I was doing with my life. I explained my situation very briefly and he then asked if I would be interested in working in association with Capernwray and told me what he had in mind. The things he mentioned were identical to the list I had drawn up a week before, though in a different order.

I had known Capernwray since first going to a teenage holiday week at the age of 13. I had worked on the staff during my school holidays one summer, had attended the year-long Bible school, and many of its leaders had become heroes to me. But I had never thought seriously of joining the staff there because I respected so highly the calibre of the existing staff that the issue just didn't enter realistically into my thinking as a possibility. On this occasion I immediately said 'Yes' to Major Thomas, to which he responded by saying I didn't need to be so hasty, should take time to think about it, and come back to see him in a few weeks' time when we would be able to make a decision. I told him of my experience a few days before that had led me to write a list of six things I thought my life should consist of, and that they were the very things he had just given to me. He laughed and said that as it looked pretty obvious there seemed no reason to hang around, and that we should backtrack to the previous midnight and say that as from then I was on Capernwray staff!

As I write this, more than a quarter of a century has passed since that day, and I have lived every day with a clear sense of being in the right place at the right time for the right purpose, whether in the evangelistic or Bible teaching programme at Capernwray Hall itself or in the wider ministry God has given in many other parts of the world, all of which were included in that original vision.

How God imparts his vision to us is his business, but it is the principle that is important. Sometimes we need to keep the vision hidden away in our hearts until the circumstances come together in such a way that makes it right to move, much as Nehemiah did when returning from the Persian capital of Susa to rebuild the city walls of Jerusalem that had been destroyed during the Babylonian conquest. He said, 'I had not told anyone what my God had put in my heart to do for Jerusalem' (Nehemiah 2:12). It is fine to have secrets between ourselves and God. Nehemiah told no one what God had put in his heart, and because God was its author, it required no manipulation on his part to bring it to pass! In the course of time the circumstances he anticipated came together and the dream was fulfilled.

Mary, the mother of Jesus, was amazed at what the shepherds had to say when they visited the stable, 'But Mary treasured up all these things and pondered them in her heart' (Luke 2:19). She kept some of the things God had shown her locked in her heart, not even explaining to Jesus' brothers and sisters, for at a crucial stage at the commencement of his ministry 'even his own brothers did not believe in him' (John 7:5). They had been as surprised and embarrassed as the rest of Nazareth when Jesus stood in the synagogue for the first time and announced himself the fulfilment of messianic prophecy! Mary was not surprised, but she had kept it in the secret recesses of her heart. We can actually destroy our vision by talking too much and too soon. The vision may be blurred around the edges, we may be unsure of detail, but if it is from God it will come to pass – without any manipulation on our part.

The future begins today

Paul tells Agrippa:

> . . . I was not disobedient to the vision from heaven. First to those in Damascus, then to those in Jerusalem and in all Judea, and to the Gentiles also, I preached that they should repent and turn to God and prove their repentance by their deeds. (Acts 26:19–20)

With a sense of his future (12–14 years ahead of its fulfilment), Paul began to preach in Damascus, right where he was. Luke records that following his meeting with Ananias 'Saul spent several days with the disciples in Damascus. At once he began to preach in the synagogues that Jesus is the Son of God' (Acts 9:19–20). He began immediately to involve himself in activity that related to his 'vision from heaven'. When we have some sense of the general direction in which God is leading and our compass is set, we must begin to move in that direction, no matter how tentatively. You don't become a missionary by arriving in a foreign country! You start at home.

I once heard a missionary leader say that the kind of people God calls to be missionaries are those most needed at home. If they are effective *here*, they will be effective *there*. If they are of little value *here*, they will be of little value *there*! This is implicit in the final words of Jesus to his disciples prior to his ascension: 'But you will receive power when the Holy Spirit comes on you; and you will be my witnesses in Jerusalem, and in all Judea and Samaria, and to the ends of the earth' (Acts 1:8). They were to be witnesses exactly where they were – Jerusalem – and the stream would flow from there to the ends of the earth. But if there is no spring there will be no stream. A friend of mine had on his desk a plaque which said simply, 'As now, so then. As here, so there.' What I am to be *there*, I must be *here*. What I am to be *then*, I must be *now*.

I knew from the age of 16 in a vague way that God was calling me to preach. With a small group of about six friends, I began to go into the coffee bars near our home to reach the young people who congregated there. We also began to preach in the open air on a Saturday afternoon and in the course of time were invited as a team to go and preach in some of the village churches and chapels around the area. By the age of 17 I spent almost every Sunday night going to small rural churches where we would sing, give testimony and one of us would preach. I have no doubt those times were crucial to our development and the confirmation of our various futures. A number of us went into full-time Christian work, and the others became, and still are, active as leaders in their own communities. Paul did not sit around waiting! The divine initiative had been taken, he had received his compass bearing, and began immediately to move in the direction the compass pointed by preaching then and there in Damascus. His message 'that Jesus is the Son of God' (Acts 9:20) may have been fairly primitive, for that may have been all he knew at this stage, but he preached it.

I knew a student who had a strong sense of calling from God to serve him in China. He had never been to China, but learned to speak Mandarin, took an interest in Chinese culture, joined a Chinese church in the city where he studied, ate in Chinese restaurants and befriended Chinese people. His compass bearing was set on China, so he did everything appropriate to reaching Chinese people in the meantime.

The fulfilment of long-term vision always begins with short-term obedience. This was true for Paul, and must remain true for every one of us.

4

Time Out with God

One of the characteristics of God is that he is never in a hurry! In fact, on the contrary, he takes his time in accomplishing his will and fulfilling promises he makes to people. He waited 25 years after promising Abraham at the age of 75 that he and his 65-year-old wife Sarah would become the parents of a baby son. He let Moses sit in the Midian desert with a handful of sheep for 40 years before calling him to lead Israel out of Egypt – at the ripe old age of 80. God is never under the pressure of time that stands as so much of a threat to human ambition and human agendas, especially in our fast-moving world of the twenty-first century. God warned Isaiah:

> Woe to those . . . who say, 'Let God hurry,
>> let him hasten his work
>> so that we may see it.
> Let it approach,
>> let the plan of the Holy One of Israel come,
>> so that we may know it.' (Isaiah 5:18–19)

In a series of curses on the people for their obvious sins and failings stands this surprising rebuke to those who say, 'Let God hurry.'

God took time to mould and mature the apostle Paul. If he was given a vision of his future from the risen Christ on the Damascus road, it was to be many years before he began to experience its fulfilment through the extensive missionary travels he subsequently undertook. It is difficult to establish an exact chronology of Paul's life during the intervening years between his conversion and first missionary journey. F.F. Bruce, one of the twentieth century's leading authorities on Paul, suggests a 14-year period between Paul's conversion and his first missionary journey.[1] Certainly it was at least a wait of twelve years. From the information available to us both in the book of Acts and in Paul's own writings (particularly Galatians), we may attempt to reconstruct that period as follows:

1. Converted in Damascus (Acts 9:1–19)
2. Preaches in Damascus for 'several days' (Acts 9:19–20)
3. Spends period of time in Arabia (Galatians 1:17)
4. Returns to Damascus for 'many days' (Galatians 1:17; Acts 9:22–23)
5. Experiences dramatic escape from Damascus (Acts 9:25; 2 Corinthians 11:32–33)
6. Goes to Jerusalem (three years after conversion) (Galatians 1:18)
7. Barnabas introduces Paul to Peter and James (Galatians 1:18–19; Acts 9:27)
8. Stays in Jerusalem for only 15 days (Galatians 1:18)
9. Travels to Tarsus via Caesarea because his life is at risk (Acts 9:30; Galatians 1:21)
10. Barnabas finds him in Tarsus and takes him to Antioch (Acts 11:22–26)

---

[1] F.F. Bruce, *Paul: Apostle of the Heart Set Free* (Eerdmans, 1979), Chronological Table, p. 475.

11. Teaches large numbers of people for one year in Antioch (Acts 11:25–26)
12. Disciples are first called 'Christians' in Antioch (Acts 11:25–26)
13. Carries a gift from Antioch to the church in Jerusalem (Acts 11:30)
14. Returns to Antioch, taking John Mark from Jerusalem (Acts 12:25)
15. Set apart as a missionary (with Barnabas) in Antioch (Acts 13:1–3)
16. First missionary journey with Barnabas and John Mark (Acts 13:4)

We have already discussed the sense of vision Paul had received from God that motivated and sustained him during these years. There are other events, however, about which we have some information that contributed to sustaining and preparing Paul during this waiting period.

Solitude in Arabia

Soon after his conversion in Damascus, and before he ever revisited Jerusalem, Paul went for a period of time to Arabia, possibly for as long as three years. He writes that, following his conversion in Damascus,

> . . . I did not consult any man, nor did I go up to Jerusalem to see those who were apostles before I was, but I went immediately into Arabia and later returned to Damascus. Then after three years, I went up to Jerusalem to get acquainted with Peter and stayed with him fifteen days. (Galatians 1:16–18)

He had spent just a few days in Damascus following his conversion, speaking in the synagogue to the astonishment of those who knew him only as the enemy from Jerusalem on a mission to cause havoc among believers in Christ. Yet here he was, advocating the very message he had come to destroy! He then left for Arabia, seemingly to be alone, to come to terms with the radical transformation that had taken place in his life, to have uninterrupted times of solitude in the Arabian wilderness, and above all to meet with the Lord Jesus Christ alone.

Ananias in Damascus could instruct and encourage him, but no human being can ever become a substitute for learning from Christ himself. This time of meeting was a very particular one, for Paul had been told by Jesus on the Damascus road that there were things 'I will show you' (Acts 26:16). Paul's claim to the Galatians is that his gospel is not second hand, for 'I did not receive it from any man, nor was I taught it; rather, I received it by revelation from Jesus Christ' (Galatians 1:12). It is most likely that when Paul refers to this 'revelation from Jesus Christ', or elsewhere to 'the mystery made known to me by revelation' (Ephesians 3:3) he is referring to encounters with the risen Christ that took place, in part at least, during this period of solitude in Arabia.

The area known as Arabia in New Testament times was much smaller than Arabia in the Old Testament, covering only the Sinai peninsula to the south of Palestine and including 'Horeb, the mountain of God'. It is the place where, many years before, both Moses and Elijah had met with God at significant times in their lives and ministries.[2] Here God had spoken to Moses in the drama of the burning bush and sent him back to Egypt to deliver Israel from the slavery to which they had been subjugated for so long. In the same spot he had caught Elijah on the run from Jezebel and in a 'gentle whisper'

---

[2] See Exodus 3:1 and 1 Kings 19:8.

called him by name and sent him back the way he had come. Moses had been called to lead Israel into a new destiny as a nation under God and to give us the first five books of Scripture. Elijah had been called as the first of a new breed of itinerant prophets whose writings would form the last 17 books of the Old Testament. Now, against the same physical landscape and under the same sky, God met with another choice servant whose unique role would be to spearhead the spread of the gospel throughout the Mediterranean world, and to contribute 13 New Testament letters for the benefit of the church to come.

The book of Acts does not record Paul's period in Arabia, and we know it only from the personal account he gave to the Galatians. The context in which he refers to the event in that letter probably helps us to understand the significance of it. He explains that it was three years after his conversion before he ever returned to Jerusalem or met with Peter, James or any of the other apostles from whom he may have learned truths about Christ. His point is that he was neither commissioned by them to be an apostle to the Gentiles nor was he schooled by them in the doctrines of the Christian faith, but had received both from the risen Christ himself. There had been of course the dramatic and pivotal revelation to him on the Damascus road, but this had its limitations, perhaps restricted in substance to the message he preached in the synagogue in Damascus immediately following his conversion, 'that Jesus is the Son of God' (Acts 9:20). There was much more detail to be learned after this and, states Paul, 'nor did I go up to Jerusalem to see those who were apostles before I was, but I went immediately into Arabia and later returned to Damascus' (Galatians 1:17). His visit to Arabia therefore is directly related in his narrative to the message that 'I received by revelation from Jesus Christ'.

'The Lord, not I', and 'I, not the Lord'

Whether this 'revelation from Jesus Christ' involved his physical ears hearing an audible voice or his inner heart receiving impressions of truth he knew to be from the Lord, he does not explain, but he is in no doubt as to the origin of what he heard: it was the Lord himself. In his later writings he several times states to the effect that 'I received from the Lord what I also passed on to you' (1 Corinthians 11:23). In one passage he sets two contrasting statements in instructions he gives about marriage, between 'I give this command (not I, but the Lord)' (1 Corinthians 7:10), and a few sentences later, 'To the rest I say this (I, not the Lord) (verse 12). It has sometimes been argued that the first statement is one he regards as divinely given and therefore authoritative, but the second is merely his own idea for which he is not willing to claim a divine mandate. It is most likely, however, that what Paul is referring to is that the first statement reflects an issue about which the Lord has specifically spoken to him at some earlier period in his life, whereas the second does not. This does not downgrade the second simply to a personal opinion of Paul. He, along with many of the writers at the time, may not have been fully aware that his words were 'God-breathed' (2 Timothy 3:16) and destined to become part of Scripture. With this hindsight we must regard Paul's second statement, 'I, not the Lord', as significant and binding as the first, 'not I, but the Lord'.

The point is that there were particular occasions when Paul claimed to have received words from the risen Christ, to such an extent that when he later met with the apostles and leaders in Jerusalem for the first time, three years after his conversion, they had no substance to add to his message. The fact that this message coincided completely with that of the apostles, who had been with Jesus personally during the years of his ministry around Galilee and Judea, only confirmed the authenticity of Paul's encounters.

The reason for our looking at Paul in this way is to enable us to discover in his experience some principles and issues that may help us in our lives some 20 centuries later. We live in an entirely different world, with different pressures, yet God's dealings with Paul and his moulding of him into a man of such remarkable influence carries its lessons for us now. There are some common principles that transcend the centuries and cultures to serve as encouragement and instruction in our own day.

We know nothing about the day-to-day details of Paul's time in Arabia, except that at its core lies an appointment with the risen Christ so that Paul might be able 'to know his will and to see the Righteous One and to hear words from his mouth' (Acts 22:14). Although details of this encounter remain unique to Paul, the principle of making time and place to 'know his will . . . and to hear words from his mouth' remains paramount for each of us who means business with God. It is true there is no fresh revelation for us to receive from God and we have no original message to give to the world, for as Paul affirmed, 'If anybody is preaching to you a gospel other than what you accepted, let him be eternally condemned!' (Galatians 1:9). But, although there is no fresh truth to receive, there must be fresh, personal encounters with God. Our message can be passed from one generation to another, but our personal experience of God can never be received from another: it has always to be first hand.

Paul had an overriding ambition that influenced every other part of his life: 'I want to know Christ and the power of his resurrection and the fellowship of sharing in his sufferings' (Philippians 3:10). Where did he obtain that? Not sitting in a pew, no matter how great and godly the person in the pulpit may be, nor in the seminary classroom at the feet of the greatest teachers available. No, this knowledge of Christ is to be found only in personal encounters with the Lord himself. I spend day after day teaching students in our Bible school, or preaching and teaching in conferences and churches all over the world, but there are certain things I know I can never teach anyone. I may point to those things, I may encourage the pursuit of them, but my students learn very little at the stage when it is only ink marks on their note paper, and the congregations I address learn very little when they have simply heard propositional truth about God.

All of this is necessary and should inspire people to do business with God personally, but it is no substitute in itself for that individual encounter and personal relationship that is the core of the Christian life. I may point a person to Christ and encourage them in the exercise of repentance and faith, but until 'The Spirit himself testifies with our spirit that we are God's children' (Romans 8:16) they have no assurance, no joy and no peace.

Relationship not scholarship

Paul said to Timothy, 'I know whom I have believed' (2 Timothy 1:12). He did not say, 'I know *what* I have believed.' There is all the difference in the world between knowing *what* we believe and knowing *whom* we believe. To be preoccupied with knowing *what* we believe is to be preoccupied with scholarship. To be preoccupied with knowing *whom* we believe is to be preoccupied with relationship. The Christian life is not about scholarship, but about relationship. Scholarship is legitimate and necessary, but must at all times be the servant of relationship. Jesus said, 'Now this is eternal life: that they may *know you*, the only true God, and Jesus Christ, whom you have sent' (John 17:3, my emphasis). To know God and to know Christ is the essence of eternal life. When knowing *what* we believe exceeds in quality and depth knowing *whom* we believe, we are to that extent not improved but impoverished.

We have today the completed revelation of God in Scripture, something Paul did not have. Our Old Testament was in circulation in Paul's day, but in cumbersome scrolls and restricted to the synagogues. Today, thanks to the invention of the printing press and now the micro chip, we can access the whole of the Scriptures, both Old and New Testaments, at any time, in a multitude of different versions and enjoy through the written word the privilege of hearing the voice of the living Word, the Lord Jesus himself. We need the Holy Spirit to enable us to understand the word, for 'The man without the Spirit does not accept the things that come from the Spirit of God, for they are foolishness to him, and he cannot understand them, because they are spiritually discerned' (1 Corinthians 2:14). Time to meet with God, time to listen to God, time to talk to God in dependency on the Holy Spirit are indispensable ingredients in our knowledge of God and growth in character and usefulness.

This is the enduring value of Paul's time in Arabia, where the foundation of his ministry to come was laid in communion with Jesus himself. How long he actually spent in Arabia we may not be sure. He spent 'a few days' in Damascus after his conversion, then went to Arabia for an unspecified period, before returning to Damascus for 'many days' and then following his escape from Damascus, went up to Jerusalem to meet with the apostles for the first time. The lapse of time between his conversion and arrival in Jerusalem was 'after three years' (Galatians 1:18). This may simply be a round figure and if so, according to the Jewish reckoning of time, would mean it included three calendar years, with at least a full year in the middle, plus parts of two other years either side. For example a period of time from December of a first year to January of a third year would be measured as 'three years' though in fact the period covers only

14 months (much as Jesus predicted he would be in the tomb for 'three days and three nights', meaning it included the three days of Friday, Saturday and Sunday, though he was literally, by our current ways of measuring time, only in the tomb for about 36 hours from Friday night to Sunday morning – two nights and one day). However, Paul states that his visit to Jerusalem was 'after three years' rather than 'in the third year' (as Jesus was raised 'on the third day' not 'after the third day') suggesting it covered a full three-year period of time.

Ecstatic encounters

We should also comment on some of the more unique encounters Paul had with God. Once he described to the Corinthians an experience that was almost certainly his own, though he described it in the third person.

> I know a man in Christ who fourteen years ago was caught up to the third heaven. Whether it was in the body or out of the body I do not know . . . He heard inexpressible things, things that man is not permitted to tell. (2 Corinthians 12:2–4)

The significance of this event isn't altogether obvious, for the tantalizing thing is that he heard things he described as being 'inexpressible' and which, had they been expressible, he was not permitted to tell anyway! Why did Paul bother to tell the Corinthians about this event when nothing of substance is disclosed from the vision? Paul was writing this in his letter to the Corinthians in the midst of a defence against specific charges brought against him that he was unspiritual.

We know from Paul's letters to Corinth that the church there veered strongly towards a preoccupation with charismatic phenomena, and attached high value to ecstatic manifestations, of which they had seen very little evidence in Paul's ministry. The apostle had tried to tone these experiences down and had, in his first letter to them, encouraged the Corinthians to restrict these to a proper perspective. By the time he wrote Second Corinthians, some in Corinth had had enough of Paul's caution and openly challenged the quality of his spirituality, to which he reluctantly feels compelled to respond in chapters 10–13. He apologizes for his boasting, but in order to address the particular charges made about him, he states after two chapters of justifying his apostleship, 'Although there is nothing to be gained, I will go on to visions and revelations from the Lord' (2 Corinthians 12:1) and in this context describes his experience of being caught up into paradise some 14 years before. This probably achieved its immediate goal of impressing some of the Corinthians whose own terms of reference demanded such experiences to validate his genuineness. But what is the longer term value of this record to us? Perhaps it has no particular value other than acknowledging the various and sometimes unique ways God speaks to particular people, something Paul knew from personal experience.

Some have attributed an element of mysticism to Paul, with his unusual visions and meetings with Christ, and there may be some substance to this. Mysticism has been defined as 'the doctrine that the individual can come into immediate contact with God through subjective experiences which differ essentially from the experience of ordinary life'.[3] Some would place Paul's conversion experience, his teaching about union with Christ, and the sharing of Christ's sufferings, as well as his more unusual visions into a mystical framework. But Paul's all-consuming passion was 'the surpassing greatness of knowing

---

[3] R.C. Tannehill, *Dying and Rising with Christ: A Study in Pauline Theology*, p. 4 (Topelmann, 1967), quoted in *Dictionary of Paul and his Letters* (IVP, 1993), p. 627.

Christ Jesus my Lord' (Philippians 3:8) which he longed for each of his readers and listeners to know for themselves on the basis that it was as fully available to them as it was to him. There were unique features of Paul's personal experience of God, as there may be for each of us, but nothing in Paul's message was regarded as unique to himself, so much so that he was able to say to the Corinthians, 'I urge you to imitate me' (1 Corinthians 4:16); and, 'Follow my example, as I follow the example of Christ' (1 Corinthians 11:1). To the Thessalonians he said, 'You became imitators of us and of the Lord' (1 Thessalonians 1:6); and to the Philippians, 'Whatever you have learned or received or heard from me, or seen in me – put it into practice' (Philippians 4:9). This is not the encouragement of someone who regarded his own knowledge of God to be unique in any way at all, but something to be imitated, followed and put into practice by other people.

We must not measure the value of our own spiritual experiences by comparing them with those of others, for of course there is variation in life's experience. We recognize the validity of varying experiences of God, as they contribute to our knowledge of God being deepened and our likeness to Christ being enhanced. This was the only valid criterion by which Paul measured the value of his own experiences. This remained true whether it involved such heights as being caught up into the third heaven and hearing inexpressible things, or such depths of spiritual experience as the debilitating thorn in his flesh, which he described unambiguously as 'a messenger from Satan, to torment me' (2 Corinthians 12:7). This led, however, to the discovery that 'My grace is sufficient for you, for my power is made perfect in weakness' (verse 9). Both of these events are recorded by Paul in the same chapter in which he is describing his personal dealings with God. He adds with satisfaction to the 'thorn in the flesh' experience, 'Therefore I will boast all the more gladly about my weaknesses, so that Christ's power may rest on me.' The value of these experiences, whether seemingly good or bad, whether coming directly from God or from Satan (as in the case of Paul's thorn), is that they drive us to know a little bit more of Jesus, and that we learn more fully to exchange our weakness for his strength.

The beginnings of opposition

Paul's time in Arabia was not spent solely in isolation or in a state of constantly receiving revelation from Christ, for he hints elsewhere that his activities provoked some opposition and set him on the run. In one of his letters to the Corinthians Paul explains an event in Damascus that took place on his return to that city from Arabia:

> the governor under King Aretas had the city of the Damascenes guarded in order to arrest me. But I was lowered in a basket from a window in the wall and slipped through his hands. (2 Corinthians 11:32–33)

King Aretas presided over the Nabatean kingdom, the territory described by Paul as Arabia, and the man described as 'the governor under King Aretas' was his representative in Damascus where many Arabians lived, and like other ethnic groups, had a representative of their government on hand. The only reason King Aretas would be intent on having Paul arrested was because he was causing trouble in Arabia. It may well be that Paul had returned to Damascus primarily because he was no longer welcome in Arabia. Paul, as was his later practice, may have sought out the synagogue in the Arabian capital Petra, and begun to preach Christ there until he sufficiently antagonized the Jews and was driven out (the book of Acts indicates that the Jews, as well as the representatives of King Aretas, wanted to arrest and kill Paul in Damascus[4]). Driven from the synagogue, as would become his normal experience in his missionary travels, Paul would no doubt have turned to the Gentiles and offered them the gospel, and perhaps it was here that he provoked the anger of King Aretas.

When Paul describes to the Corinthians the catalogue of persecutions he has endured in his ministry, his imprisonments, his floggings, his exposure to death, the 39 stripes, the beating with rods, the stoning, the shipwrecks, the dangers from rivers, from bandits, from Jews, from Gentiles, in the cities, in the country, at sea, from false brothers, his days of sleeplessness, of hunger and nakedness (see 2 Corinthians 11:23–28), he is no doubt looking back to his time in Arabia as well as his better known missionary journeys. There he did his apprenticeship and learned to preach, fighting for truth and learning through the hardness of his circumstances the promise he gave to Timothy many years later, as he neared the end of his life: 'everyone who wants to live a godly life in Christ Jesus will be persecuted' (2 Timothy 3:12). Paul knew exactly what he was talking about, for from his earliest days as a believer in Jesus Christ, this had been his lot!

---

[4] Compare Acts 9:23–25 with 2 Corinthians 11:32.

5

The Value of a Friend

The apostle Paul's genius for friendship is well documented. We can compile a list of around 70 names of people in the New Testament about whom we would never have heard but for their association with Paul. Paul was one of those men who attracted friends and colleagues like a magnet attracts iron filings. However, in the circle of friends that surrounded the apostle Paul, none was so valuable to him and so significant in his own personal development as Barnabas, his longest Christian friend. The two almost certainly first encountered each other before Paul was converted on the Damascus road, for while Paul was participating in the persecution of the believers in Jerusalem following the martyrdom of Stephen, Barnabas was developing as a recognized influence for good in the Jerusalem church. How long he had been in Jerusalem we do not know, for although he was of the Jewish tribe of Levi, he was a native of Cyprus from where at some point he had migrated back to Jerusalem.

He is described as an apostle in later years, and it is most probable that Barnabas was present in Jerusalem for some time during the ministry of Jesus. No doubt he listened to his teaching, and had perhaps even witnessed his crucifixion. He could well have been among the 120 people awaiting the gift of the Holy Spirit on the Day of Pentecost. An early tradition says that Barnabas was one of the 70 sent out by Jesus (see Luke10), but this is impossible to confirm.

The name 'Barnabas' was actually a nickname given him by the apostles in Jerusalem. His real name was Joseph, but he was called Barnabas, meaning 'son of encouragement', because of the spirit of generosity and encouragement that characterized him. Barnabas owned land and participated in a practice, spreading among the landowning believers in Jerusalem, of selling land and donating the proceeds to the apostles to use as they thought best. He had family connections in Jerusalem, for his cousin John Mark lived there with his mother, Mary, who hosted the Jerusalem church in her home. This may explain why, following the martyrdom of Stephen when 'all except the apostles were scattered throughout Judea and Samaria' (Acts 8:1), Barnabas stayed in Jerusalem, perhaps at the home of his aunt and cousin. At this time he was probably not recognized as an apostle, for he is not described as such until he and Paul are on their first missionary journey (see Acts 14:14) some 15 years or so later.

When Paul came to Jerusalem for the first time after his conversion in Damascus and subsequent stay in Arabia, the apostles were reluctant to trust him or even to meet with him. They had last known him when he wrought havoc in the Jerusalem church, and their relief that he had left them three years ago had only been tempered by the fact he had set off for Damascus to cause as much trouble for the believers there. They picked up rumours that filtered through from Damascus that he 'who formerly persecuted us is now preaching the faith he once tried to destroy' (Galatians 1:23). Clearly they had found it difficult to attach much credibility to the story, however, for when Paul eventually returned, 'they were all afraid of him, not believing that he really was a disciple' (Acts 9:26). If any real credibility was to be established, someone would need to go out on a limb. It would take courage to reach out to Paul and run the risk that all their fears would be found to be true. The one who chose to take that risk was Barnabas:

> But Barnabas took him and brought him to the apostles. He told them how Saul on his journey had seen the Lord and that the Lord had spoken to him, and how in Damascus he had preached fearlessly in the name of Jesus. (Acts 9:27)

Barnabas not only befriended him but became his spokesman, explaining and persuading the rest of the disciples in Jerusalem that he was to be trusted. 'So Saul stayed with them and moved about freely in Jerusalem, speaking boldly in the name of the Lord' (Acts 9:28).

When Paul wrote what has become one of the most profound descriptions of love in all of literature, I wonder if he was thinking of Barnabas: 'Love . . . keeps no record of wrongs . . . It always protects, always trusts, always hopes, always perseveres. Love never fails' (1 Corinthians 13:4–8). Barnabas protected Paul, trusted Paul, placed his hopes in Paul, and persevered with Paul. If we may later thank Paul for Timothy and the investment of time, patience, love and example that brought Timothy to maturity, we must equally thank Barnabas for Paul, for without his role Paul may never have had the opportunities he had to develop as he did.

Having gained acceptance in Jerusalem, Paul was at liberty to preach, but within two weeks had provoked such opposition that he had to flee the city when the Jews tried to kill him. He was well known to the Jews, and had been something of a hero in the cause of crushing the infant church three years previously. Now he was back, preaching again in his familiar synagogues, but a different message was coming from his lips! His former colleagues were not impressed.

The apostles decided that for his own safety he should be sent home to Tarsus for a period of time, so they took him down to Caesarea, put him on a boat and he sailed off into a decade of obscurity. No doubt he initially rejoined his family in Tarsus. When Paul had last left Tarsus he would have been the pride of his family. With his brilliant mind and his skills as a leader of men they had grounds to hold high hopes for him. He was climbing the ladder of his chosen profession faster than any of his contemporaries. In fact, he later claimed, 'I was advancing in Judaism beyond many Jews of my own age and was extremely zealous for the traditions of my fathers' (Galatians 1:14). His parents had no doubt been keen themselves to serve God in the only way they knew by keeping the law, and would have fully endorsed Paul's stance of opposition to the new movement gripping Jerusalem. Now he was returning home as a convert to the very cause he had opposed.

Paul described himself as 'from Tarsus in Cilicia, a citizen of no ordinary city' (Acts 21:39), perhaps implying his own family's status there. Citizenship in Tarsus was not by right of birth but was dependent on the ownership of a certain amount of property. Although Jewish, his family had also been granted the privilege of Roman citizenship, and this gave certain rights which Paul several times availed himself of during his apostolic career, such as the right to a fair trial, the right to appeal to the emperor of Rome if the jurisdiction of a lower court was thought to be unjust, and exemption from some of the more barbaric forms of punishment for which Rome was famous.

Paul no doubt was welcomed back home as the son of a respected family. As a Jew living in Tarsus, his family probably lived among other Jews, as such towns normally had their ethnic sections. We may discern Paul's tactic in the Jewish community in Tarsus as

> To the Jews I became like a Jew, to win the Jews. To those under the law I became like one under the law (though I myself am not under the law), so as to win those under the law. (1 Corinthians 9:20)

It is much more difficult to unlearn and correct a wrong understanding than it is to learn something new. If an initial approach threaten what people hold dear, they instinctively fight to retain it, as Paul himself had done in Jerusalem. If, however, something positive and more attractive is made available, which does not in the first instance seem to threaten what is already held, once the new has been embraced, the old begins to take on a different significance and in due time falls away of its own accord.

As Paul's own experience had taught him, it was when he met Christ and experienced a transformation of his own life that he began to see his Judaism in a new light, and could start to leave it behind. Prior to his encounter with Christ, any attempt to take away the demands of the law from Paul would only have resulted in its most severe defence. It is true that for Jewish converts, once the truth of the gospel of Jesus Christ has been embraced, there has to develop a proper understanding of the implications of the gospel in relation to the observation of the many laws of the Old Covenant. Paul was adamant in following this through, and wrote to the 'foolish Galatians' who having been *saved by faith* in Christ alone had not understood the implications of *living by faith* in Christ alone, rather than continuing to live under the rigorous demands of the law.

Back in Tarsus Paul would not have flaunted his liberty in Christ. He would have lived as a Jew, and placed himself under the requirements of the law, not any more as a means to salvation, but as a bridge over which he might travel to his fellow Jews. It would only be a matter of time, however, before Paul would be recognized as holding the truths about liberty in Christ for which he really stood. On his missionary journeys he would begin to preach where possible in synagogues of the Jewish Diaspora. For a number of weeks – sometimes for as long as three months – he would be welcomed back each Sabbath day to say more, until his words began to hit home and people began to understand their full implication. It was then that he would be driven out of the synagogue and the inevitable round of persecutions would begin. This pattern seems to have taken place on his early visit to Arabia soon after his conversion, and no doubt took place again on his home turf in Tarsus. When Paul listed in his writings the catalogue of persecutions he had had to endure it is likely that some refer to this period in Tarsus (see 2 Corinthians 11:23ff.).

It may have been here in Tarsus that he experienced the out-of-body experience he describes in 2 Corinthians 12:2–4. If there is any similarity in this vision of heaven with John's experience on the isle of Patmos, where he too was caught up to heaven after a voice invited him, 'Come up here, and I will show you what must take place after this' (Revelation 4:1–2), the contrast is more significant than the similarity. John was told to write what he had seen, but Paul was not permitted to say anything. John's revelation was given at a time of persecution against the church, giving his early readers faith in God, a confidence in their message and an assurance about the future despite the present hardships they faced. Perhaps Paul's vision too was a source of encouragement to him in a time of loneliness, opposition and ostracism, where a vision of heaven had the effect of reinvigorating and fortifying him for the work yet to be done.

Despite the length of time Paul spent in Tarsus, there is no record of a church being established there, no letter sent to any believer there, and no attempt to include Tarsus on a missionary journey, though Paul may well have passed through the region on his way from Antioch to Galatia at the beginning of his second missionary journey. Perhaps the lack of converts in Tarsus was due to similar reasons for lack of disciples in Nazareth, where Jesus explained that 'a prophet has no honour in his own country' (John 4:44). However, for whatever reason Paul seemed to make little headway in Tarsus and surrounding areas. The vision he had been given on the Damascus road and again from Ananias when he had come to lay hands on him – 'This man is my chosen instrument to carry my name before the Gentiles and their kings and before the people of Israel' (Acts 9:15) – did not seem to be fulfilled in Tarsus. Where were the kings? Where was the significant response to be expected from the Gentile communities to whom he preached? So far the original vision, to which he had remained obedient, was not being fulfilled in the terms he had been given reason to expect, and Paul, now in his forties, might expect to be at the zenith of his powers.

Meanwhile, during this long period in Tarsus, marvellous growth was taking place in the church in Judea and its surrounding areas and provinces. Most significant was the turning to Christ of both Jew and Gentile in the city of Antioch in Syria, 400 miles north of Jerusalem. Antioch was a city of around 300,000 people and one of the most important cities in the Roman Empire. It had a very large Jewish population (variously estimated as between 22,000 and 65,000). Following the death of Stephen, in which Paul had played such an ignoble part, some of the believers had scattered to Antioch and begun to preach the gospel not only to Jews but also to Greeks. This was the first concerted outreach to Gentiles and a great number of both Jews and Greeks believed and turned to the Lord. When the elders in Jerusalem heard this good news they sent Barnabas to Antioch to consolidate and advance the work. This he evidently did with great success. While in Antioch Barnabas remembered again his friend Paul, and needing help in his work, set off to Tarsus to find Paul to bring him back as his assistant.

Paul spent a year with Barnabas in Antioch, a time of much growth and significant impact. Outside Jerusalem no church played so large a part in the growth of the early church as did the church in Antioch, where the disciples 'were called Christians first' (Acts 11:26). From Antioch help was sent to the church in Jerusalem to assist it during the severe famine that took place in the reign of Claudius. Perhaps most significantly of all, the first formal missionary journey to the Gentile world set out from Antioch, not Jerusalem. Believers had already scattered to places as far away as Rome and churches had already been established in many regions, but no official apostolic envoys had been sent until the leaders of the church in Antioch were instructed by the Holy Spirit to 'Set apart for me Barnabas and Saul for the work to which I have called them' (Acts 13:2).

Encouraging younger men and women

The friendship of Barnabas sought out Paul and brought him back into the mainstream of activity. Luke's thumbnail sketch of Barnabas in Antioch is as high a tribute as could be paid to any man: 'He was a good man, full of the Holy Spirit and faith, and a great number of people were brought to the Lord' (Acts 11:24). He was good; he was full of the Holy Spirit; he was full of faith; he brought people to Christ. What higher and more noble aspiration could anyone have? But as a good man would, he looked for opportunities to bring younger men into the sphere of his ministry. He was not feathering his own nest, or establishing his own reputation, or building his own church, or setting up his own empire. Instead, he was a man caught up exclusively in the interests of Jesus Christ, and therefore Jesus Christ's interest in the younger Paul became Barnabas' interest too.

The encouragement of younger Christians by older ones is vital to their wholesome development. Young people do not have the experience or wisdom that age brings, but they need the nurturing, encouragement and the willingness of older people to step aside and make way for them. Paul experienced this in full from Barnabas, but it was something Paul's protégé Timothy did not find in Ephesus, provoking Paul to write to him, 'Don't let anyone look down on you because you are young' (1 Timothy 4:12). I well remember that as a young Christian keen to serve God, one of my biggest discouragements came from older Christians who seemed to block every initiative I or my friends wished to take; who would very quickly tell us what we were doing wrong, but rarely if ever encouraged us in what we were doing right. They failed to recognize in our clumsy enthusiasm and impractical ideas, a motive to reach other young people for Christ. Where we were unwise we would have welcomed correction and advice, but some of those who should have been Barnabases to us, seemed to do anything but encourage. I shall be eternally grateful to the one or two older people who did take me aside and encourage me, pray for me and help me keep on track, but those who should have done so, failed to. Self-interest is the root of jealousy, and some older Christians who have enjoyed being at the centre of things become defensive of their own position and role, and fail to prepare the next generation well – but not Barnabas, and in turn, not Paul.

Older women too, Paul tells Titus, are to take an interest in and 'train the younger women' (Titus 2:4). Young people need the protection and wisdom of older people, and older people need the enthusiasm and adventurous spirit of younger people, without a sense of jealousy getting in the way. Barnabas was an encourager *par excellence* of younger men, and Paul was fortunate to have him as his friend at such a crucial time in his development.

When the church in Antioch provided a gift for the church in Jerusalem to help the believers there through the difficult famine they were experiencing, they decided to send it by Barnabas and Paul. The church in Judea was going through turmoil at this time. The apostle James had been put to death by Herod, then Herod himself had been struck dead when after a public address to his people he accepted the accolade 'This is the voice of a god, not of a man' (Acts 12:22). But through all this drama and turmoil 'the word of God continued to increase and spread'.

When Barnabas and Paul concluded their mission of taking relief to Jerusalem they returned to Antioch with Barnabas' cousin John Mark. Then they were set apart and commissioned for their first missionary journey.

At first Luke's account reports the pair as 'Barnabas and Saul'. Barnabas was the leader and Paul his second man, with John Mark the junior assistant on the team. They began their journey by visiting Barnabas' home region of Cyprus, from where they sailed to Pamphylia and worked through that area of southern Galatia. In Lystra they were worshipped as gods one moment, then Paul was stoned and left for dead the next. As the journey continues the narrative changes significantly from documenting the activities of 'Barnabas and Paul' to those of 'Paul and Barnabas'. Paul's leadership ability and preaching and debating skills were making him more prominent than

Barnabas, so much so that when they got to Lystra, Paul was openly recognized as the chief speaker. Barnabas didn't challenge it, or seek to restrict Paul so as to preserve his own reputation, but as he had always done, he pushed his protégé forward and encouraged him in his evident gifts of ministry, no doubt deriving great pleasure from the growth of his remarkable companion.

This is a good friend! How much Paul owed to the outstanding friendship of Barnabas we can only surmise, but from every human standpoint, had there been no Barnabas there would have been no Paul – certainly not as we know him.

6

Finding and Doing the Will of God

The fact that God has a plan for the lives of his people is one of the most reassuring aspects of the Christian life, yet to many of us one of its most troubling. It is reassuring because the idea of our short lives on earth fulfilling an eternal purpose gives a deep sense of significance and security to anyone believing it. On the other hand, it is troubling because if this really is the case, why does it seem so notoriously difficult to find and enjoy this plan with confidence? Added to that, why does obedience to the will of God not create an environment that enables us to avoid so many of the hardships, difficulties and sufferings that are common to humanity as a whole?

The apostle Paul certainly held the belief that his life and vocation were preordained, for he writes of 'God, who set me apart from birth' (Galatians 1:15). He was not just set apart from the time of his dramatic experience with Christ, and the ensuing transformation that created in him an interest in the will of God, but was set apart 'from birth', long before the Damascus road encounter. Life for Paul was not a haphazard affair at all, but one steered and directed in fulfilment of the will of God. He lived with a sense of divine co-ordination and purpose in all his movements and activities. 'I am an apostle', he consistently reminded his readers, 'by the will of God.'[1] He hadn't been looking for a job in contemporary religion, predicting the burgeoning growth of the new Christian movement and the decline of formal and established Judaism, so jumping ship and joining with Christ to further his own prospects! He was not driven by the demands of a private agenda, but was simply carrying out orders as 'a servant of Christ Jesus, called to be an apostle' (Romans 1:1).

With the antiquity of history, and the brevity of the records available to us, we are in danger of compressing Paul's whole lifetime into a few paragraphs, with all the pieces of the jigsaw falling easily into place, much as we would like our own lives to be. But this would be to read Paul with one eye closed. The will of God in our lives is always clearer in retrospect than it is in prospect. The pattern is always easier to discern and explain looking back over past events, than in looking forward to prospective events. Paul himself taught that what we see and discern is itself so unreliable that the approach of the Christian is that 'We live by faith, not by sight' (2 Corinthians 5:7). Our confidence lies more in the hidden and the unseen than in the seen and obvious.

I will attempt to answer from Paul's life and writings an important question regarding our own lives: How do we know and fulfil God's plan? How did Paul discern what the will of God was? We lesser mortals often feel a handicap in a subconscious assumption that men of Paul's stature probably enjoyed a more immediate sense of the divine will than is our own experience. We may learn broad principles of God's will for his people from Paul's writings, but we often feel there is little of the down-to-earth practical calibre that helps us confidently

---

[1] See, for example, 1 Corinthians 1:1; 2 Corinthians 1:1; Ephesians 1:1; Colossians 1:1; 2 Timothy 1:1.

find and do God's will in the nitty-gritty of contemporary life. But this would not be a fair conclusion. Paul knew the struggles and uncertainties of detail that we too experience, yet he was confident of certain fundamental issues from which the personal will of God derives.

Obedience to God's general will makes possible the discovery of his specific will for us

Before we are likely to be confident of God's specific plans for our lives, we have to be interested in God's general plans for all of his people. The truth is that probably 95 per cent of God's will for our personal lives is found in the Scriptures in the revelation of his general will for all his people. Obedience to the general will of God is the only legitimate context for the discovery of the specific will of God. Paul passed on to the Colossians the concern of his friend Epaphras, 'that you may stand firm in all the will of God' (Colossians 4:12). This standing firm in 'all the will of God' is a key ingredient. God is not the supreme employment agency whose primary purpose is to give us a decent vocation in life. What we *do* is only a secondary issue in the will of God. What we *are* is of far more importance, and our *being* provides the root and reason for our *doing*. For example, God is more concerned with *how* we drive our cars than in *which* car we drive; *how* we live at home than *which* house we live in. It may be true that God is concerned that we live in a particular house or drive a particular car, but it is secondary to his prime purpose, which is to express the character of his Son in us.

God's will – the fullness of the Holy Spirit

Writing to the Ephesians Paul tells them, 'Therefore do not be foolish, but understand what the Lord's will is' (Ephesians

5:17). That the will of God is accessible is assumed by his statement that not to understand the Lord's will is to be foolish. In that context, he immediately goes on to say, 'Do not get drunk on wine, which leads to debauchery. Instead, be filled with the Spirit.' The will of God begins with the fullness of the Spirit. The fullness of the Spirit is not the mountain peak of Christian experience, the top rung of the ladder; it is in fact a bottom rung, the position from which a life lived in the will of God begins and develops. There will almost certainly be a mountain to climb thereafter, but in order to fulfil the will of God the fullness of the Spirit is an indispensable ingredient. The command may equally be read in the present continuous tense – 'Be *being filled* with the Spirit' – not merely as an experience upon which we look back, but as a continuous condition of life to be enjoyed afresh every day. The fullness of the Spirit was foundational in Paul's own life and experience of God. In Damascus, Paul was blinded after his encounter with Christ on the road outside the city. Ananias came to visit him and, laying his hands on him, said, 'Brother Saul, the Lord – Jesus, who appeared to you on the road as you were coming here – has sent me so that you may see again and be filled with the Holy Spirit' (Acts 9:17). It is to the immense poverty of the church that we have seen the fullness of the Holy Spirit as an 'extra' to salvation rather than as the prime object of salvation. We are reconciled to God in order that he may fill our lives with himself and so lay down the only legitimate foundation for a life of usefulness and service. The ongoing fullness of the Spirit is therefore an essential criterion for enjoying the will of God.

God's will – our sanctification

To the Thessalonians Paul writes, 'It is God's will that you should be sanctified' (1 Thessalonians 4:3). If someone asks the question 'What is God's will for my life?' part of the answer must be, 'It is God's will that you should be sanctified.' This again is not directly about conduct, *doing*, but about character, *being*. The quality and nature of our conduct grows out of the quality of our character.

The word 'sanctification' contains a simple idea: to set something apart for the purpose for which it exists. For example, to sanctify a pen is to write with it – that is the purpose for which it was brought into existence. If I use my pen to stir my coffee it is not being sanctified. To sanctify a car is to drive it down the road. To keep chickens in it does not sanctify the car! Chickens may like its comfort and find it convenient to lay their eggs in the glove compartment, but that is not the purpose for which the car was manufactured and is therefore an unsanctified use of the car. When Paul states that the will of God is our sanctification, it is that we find the purpose of our existence and live accordingly.

The connotation of holiness in our contemporary usage is to be 'squeaky clean'. Cleanliness is an aspect and consequence of true holiness, but the word 'holy' means literally to be 'set apart'. When ascribed to God it is in acknowledgement of his uniqueness. He is wholly different and set apart from the creation of which he is the Creator. In itself the designation 'holy' says nothing specific about his character. When ascribed to human beings in the New Testament it is to those who have been set apart to Christ for 'the sanctifying work of the Spirit' (2 Thessalonians 2:13). The *sanctifying work of the Spirit* makes possible that for which we were created in the first place: to be a physical and visible expression of the moral character of God.

The ultimate description of God's moral character is surely found in John's statement 'God is love' (1 John 4:8). Not only is God loving; he *is* love. It is the very nature of his being. Therefore, having been created in his image we should expect this to be the ultimate expression of his purpose for us – both in terms of our love for God and of our love for one another. When asked to name the greatest commandment Jesus replied:

> 'Love the Lord your God with all your heart and with all your soul and with all your mind and with all your strength.' The second is this: 'Love your neighbour as yourself.' There is no commandment greater than these. (Mark 12:30–31)

There is no higher expression of God's image in human experience than love, and therefore we may conclude that love is the highest expression of our sanctification. That is why Paul writes in his classic description of love that apart from the motivation of love behind all we are and do, 'I am nothing' and 'I gain nothing' (1 Corinthians 13:2–3). He describes love not in abstract terms but in such a way that it may be personalized. To illustrate this, if we replace the word 'love' with the name 'Christ' the statements make just as much sense:

> Love [Christ] is patient, love [Christ] is kind. It [He] does not envy, it [he] does not boast, it [he] is not proud. It [He] is not rude, it [he] is not self-seeking, it [he] is not easily angered, it [he] keeps no record of wrongs. Love [Christ] does not delight in evil but rejoices with the truth. It [He] always protects, always trusts, always hopes, always perseveres.
> Love [Christ] never fails. (1 Corinthians 13:4–8)

This description of Christ is of the one who was 'the image of the invisible God' (Colossians 1:15), a description formerly ascribed to Adam and that defines God's creative purpose for every human being. The big challenge therefore regarding our sanctification is found in whether we can take out the word 'love' in this passage, replace it with our own name, and find the statement still makes sense! Everything else that is the will of God for us grows out of this, for it is the practical expression of the image and righteousness of God – it is the measure of our sanctification.

God's will – our gratitude

Another of Paul's statements about the general will of God is for us to 'give thanks in all circumstances, for this is God's will for you in Christ Jesus' (1 Thessalonians 5:18). If you want to do the will of God, 'give thanks in all circumstances'. This doesn't seem particularly exciting! It may even sound masochistic. We must ask the question 'For *what* must we give thanks? And to *whom* must we give thanks?'

Paul makes similar statements elsewhere. To the Philippians he says, 'Do not be anxious about anything, but in everything, by prayer and petition, with thanksgiving, present your requests to God' (Philippians 4:6). Instead of experiencing anxiety, pray with thanksgiving. This is not to be thankful *for* the difficulties, but to be thankful to God for *himself in* the difficulties. To be thankful is to acknowledge dependence. The will of God for us is that we relate everything, whether good or bad, to him in an attitude of dependency expressed by our thankfulness. We are not asked to be thankful *for* the problems we encounter, but to be thankful to God for his own presence and sufficiency *in* the problems that may threaten us. What may be a cause of anxiety to us is never a cause of anxiety to him, and in him is our security. This is to permeate everything we do: 'And whatever you do, whether in word or deed, do it all in the name of the Lord Jesus, giving thanks to God the Father through him' (Colossians 3:17).

We are not going to enjoy the specific will of God for ourselves outside a deep commitment to the general will of God for all people. In fact, we may go so far as to say that to live with a concern for the general will of God is largely to take care of the specific details of God's plan for us, for they will fall into place quite naturally – as they did for Paul.

God confirms individual vision through the church

In an earlier chapter we talked about Paul's claim to King Agrippa, 'I was not disobedient to the vision from heaven' (Acts 26:19). This 'vision from heaven' was given him in embryo form on the Damascus road. For many years, however, the full implications of it were not fully realized. It is true that Paul got on with the task of preaching Christ in Damascus, Tarsus and Antioch, but it was not until the Holy Spirit revealed the same things to the elders of the church in Antioch that had already been revealed to Paul some 12 to 14 years earlier following his conversion, that the vision began to be fulfilled. The book of Acts states:

> In the church at Antioch there were prophets and teachers: Barnabas, Simeon called Niger, Lucius of Cyrene, Manaen (who had been brought up with Herod the tetrarch) and Saul. While they were worshipping the Lord and fasting, the Holy Spirit said, 'Set apart for me Barnabas and Saul for the work to which I have called them.' (Acts 13:1–2)

An important check and balance to our own subjective sense of direction is the direction God gives to those to whom we may have an accountability. We are not intended to live the Christian life as individuals each doing our own thing for God, like 'lone rangers', but having been incorporated into his own body, the church, there must exist both a mutual respect for each other's individuality along with a mutual spirit of dependency on one another.

It was not merely the opinion of the elders in Antioch that Paul and Barnabas would make fine missionaries, but it was something the Holy Spirit said to them as they waited on him in a spirit of humility (the significance of fasting) for his instructions that were to be understood apart from any prejudices of their own. What the Holy Spirit told the elders in Antioch about Paul during their time of worship and fasting was entirely consistent with what God had told Paul so many years earlier. Incidentally, it must have taken some courage for the elders in Antioch to recognize this word from God, for Paul and Barnabas were clearly the most gifted leaders in the church, and their being sent away from Antioch on foreign missionary tours would have been to the great disadvantage of the church in Antioch itself. The idea that the people God calls to the mission field are the ones most needed at home was certainly true in Antioch.

Interestingly, on the one hand we are told that 'they [the church in Antioch] placed their hands on them and sent them off' (Acts 13:3), and on the other that they were 'sent on their way by the Holy Spirit' (Acts 13:4). Was it the church in Antioch or the Holy Spirit who sent Paul and Barnabas on their journey? John Stott wisely comments:

> Would it not be true to say both that the Spirit sent them out, by instructing the church to do so, and that the church sent them out, having been directed by the Spirit to do so? This balance will be a healthy corrective to opposite extremes. The first is the tendency to individualism, by which a Christian claims direct personal guidance by the Spirit without any reference to the church. The second is the tendency to institutionalism, by which all decision making is done by the church without any reference to the Spirit.[2]

---

[2] John R.W. Stott, *The Message of Acts* (IVP, 1994), pp. 217–18.

For this to take place, particularly in the realm of Christian service, it should not only be individual Christians who are asking, 'What is your will for my life?', but church leaders who should be asking, 'Who in this congregation are you calling to full-time ministry? Who are you calling to teach in Sunday school, to work with youth, to run a Bible class, to go to the mission field?' Paul and Barnabas did not volunteer for missionary service. Neither were they doing 'their own thing'. The initiative for their ministry was with the Holy Spirit, but having called them personally, he confirmed that calling by speaking separately to the church in Antioch, who then became the commissioning body that recognized God's call on the lives of these two men. There needs to be both the individual and the church listening to God. To outline the needs to be filled and then wait for volunteers may seem a practical way to proceed, but it opens doors to the people who may not be acting on divine initiative. That then becomes enormously difficult to correct. Sometimes we may wait for years before God confirms to one what he has already shown to another, as was true in Paul's case, but in the right time God will do so, and there can be a moving forwards with confidence.

We need to move in the obvious direction

When Paul and Barnabas set off there is no indication of how they knew where to go. Their first journey took them initially to Cyprus, which may have been an obvious move, not only because of its geographical proximity to Antioch, but because Barnabas had come from there. As mentioned earlier, God gives us not so much a blueprint of his will, as a compass. We like to think of a detailed map pinned to the wall that we can keep consulting to see where we are on the chart, what the next step is to be, and how everything is going to work out. God rarely gives us such detail. Instead, he sets our compass bearing, and having established the general direction in which he is leading us, we move out in that direction. Then we can look back over our shoulders and say with Abraham's servant, 'I being in the way, the Lord led me' (Genesis 24:27, AV). Being 'in the way' means that we are doing all we know, of all that we know! What we don't as yet know will work its way into our lives as we need it.

One important principle in following the compass bearing God has given us is not to wait around for a green light to keep beckoning us forward, but to keep going in the obvious direction until we reach a red light that stops us. The only time Paul is recorded as being confused about where to go, was one occasion on his second missionary journey when he ran into red lights, lit up by the Holy Spirit:

> Paul and his companions travelled throughout the region of Phrygia and Galatia, having been kept by the Holy Spirit from preaching the word in the province of Asia. When they came to the border of Mysia, they tried to enter Bithynia, but the Spirit of Jesus would not allow them to. So they passed by Mysia and went down to Troas. During the night Paul had a vision of a man of Macedonia standing and begging him, 'Come over to Macedonia and help us.' After Paul had seen the vision, we got ready at once to leave for Macedonia, concluding that God had called us to preach the gospel to them. (Acts 16:6–10)

Having his road to the province of Asia blocked, it seemed logical to Paul to turn to Bithynia, but when that was blocked he concluded that the only road open to them was to go on to Troas. Clearly Paul was confused. He was not really sure where he should be going. His logical understanding of things had convinced him it was sensible to go either to Asia or to Bithynia, when in his confused state he had a vision of a man of Macedonia begging him to go there instead. It was this vision, calling him in an entirely new direction, that brought Paul into Europe for the first time.

A statement in the book of Isaiah contains an important principle regarding God's intervention in our lives: 'Whether you turn to the right or to the left, your ears will hear a voice behind you, saying, "This is the way; walk in it"' (Isaiah 30:21). The voice does not come from in front, encouraging us with every sensible step we make. If we are moving in the right direction we may go for many years without any conscious sense of God's specific guidance – simply because we are on track and don't need it. When we go wrong, however, the voice comes from behind, saying, 'This is the way; walk in it.' Why did God promise a voice from 'behind'? Because it is only when the people have gone wrong that they will need to hear a voice calling them back and putting them on the right road.

God is not obligated to tell us what he is doing

There may be occasions in our lives when we have no objective confirmation at all of the will of God. God promises to guide us, but he does not promise to tell us *how*, *why* and *for what purpose*. Solomon writes, 'In all your ways acknowledge him, and he will make your paths straight' (Proverbs 3:6). This is an undertaking God has promised each of us, whether we are able to see and interpret his plan or not.

Paul spent a number of years in prison following his third missionary journey. He was arrested in Jerusalem and taken to Caesarea, where he remained imprisoned for two years before appealing to Caesar and being transported to Rome. His journey to Rome was full of adventure, with storms and a ship-wreck that left him stranded in Malta for the last three months of the winter. When he eventually arrived in Rome, Caesar was not interested in hearing his case, so the book of Acts ends with the unsatisfactory situation of Paul being held in Rome for two years awaiting the hope of a trial. For some of that time he was under house arrest with a measure of freedom, but for other parts was clearly imprisoned and in chains. His prison epistles (Ephesians, Philippians, Colossians and Philemon) were probably written during this time and describe prison conditions. However, when writing from prison to the Philippians he says, 'I am put here for the defence of the gospel' (Philippians 1:16). His being in prison was not a case of things going wrong but of being *put* there. But by whom? He describes himself to the Ephesians as 'I, Paul, the prisoner of Christ Jesus for the sake of you Gentiles' (Ephesians 3:1). It is Jesus Christ who *put* him there, and with his eyes open and alert to the opportunities around him he could say:

> Now I want you to know, brothers, that what has happened to me has really served to advance the gospel. As a result, it has become clear throughout the whole palace guard and to everyone else that I am in chains for Christ. (Philippians 1:12–13)

God does not tell us in advance what his good purposes are, but even when bad things take place in our lives (Paul was originally arrested in Jerusalem as a result of gossip passed about him by believing Jews) God works out his purposes, and we, like Paul, must trust him for that.

God generally calls us positively – *to* things not *from* things

When Paul was returning to Jerusalem at the end of his third missionary journey he had been warned that trouble awaited him there and was advised not to go. He was even encouraged to give up his journey through a prophetic utterance given by

Agabus, and his colleagues 'pleaded with Paul not to go up to Jerusalem' (Acts 21:12). But he resisted all such words of advice on the following grounds:

> And now, compelled by the Spirit, I am going to Jerusalem, not knowing what will happen to me there. I only know that in every city the Holy Spirit warns me that prison and hardships are facing me. (Acts 20:22–23)

When he eventually got to Jerusalem that is exactly what he faced, leading to his years of imprisonment in Caesarea and Rome.

The advice offered to Paul would have been easy to take. It made sense to avoid persecution, hardships, imprisonment and suffering. There are often compelling reasons to leave a situation. Life has its tough dimensions no matter who we are or where we live. The temptation to move on, to change our location, to go elsewhere is never far away when things are tough. As a general principle it is wise to discern the will of God positively rather than negatively. God calls us *to* things rather than *from* things. Paul's attitude to the situation facing him in Jerusalem was 'compelled by the Spirit, I am going to Jerusalem'. God who called him *to* Jerusalem would need to call him *to* somewhere else if this was no longer his will. But Paul would not leave his course of direction just because it was going to be hard and costly. Like the Lord Jesus before him, 'when the time was come that he should be received up, he stedfastly set his face to go to Jerusalem' (Luke 9:51, AV), so Paul resolved that there should be no turning back unless the Holy Spirit altered his direction.

These principles of discerning God's direction in Paul's life remain fundamental in our discerning of God's will in our lives:

- His specific will is found within his general will, and it is our obedience to the general will of God that must be our first priority and the context in which we discover his particular will.
- God will confirm to the wider body of the church (provided it is listening to him) what he shows us individually in relation to his calling and equipping us personally.
- We need to move actively in what seems to be the obvious direction. You can only steer a moving car.
- God does not always tell us what he is doing, for 'we walk by faith, not by sight' (2 Corinthians 5:7, AV), so we may often be unable to give an explanation of what he is doing in our lives.
- Lastly, as a general rule, God guides us positively – he calls us *to* things rather than, negatively, *from* things.

7

A Strategy for Evangelism

By whatever criteria we measure effectiveness in ministry, Paul was effective! People were converted to Christ in huge numbers, churches were established all around the Mediterranean world, and opposition was constant. Paul and his colleagues gained a reputation midway through their second missionary journey as 'These men who have caused trouble all over the world' (Acts 17:6), or 'have turned the world upside down' (AV). What to his opponents was the negative notion of 'trouble' was to Paul the positive expression of 'triumph'. People and societies were being revolutionized by his message.

The effectiveness of Paul's evangelism was not just a consequence of his divine calling, his many spiritual gifts and his enabling by God, but also of careful planning and deliberate strategy that he thought through and followed. The fact that Paul followed a clear and deliberate strategy is evident from his explanation to the Romans that his proposed visit to them would be fairly casual while en route to Spain, for Rome itself was not part of his strategy because it lay outside his sense of personal calling: 'It has always been my ambition to preach the gospel where Christ was not known, so that I would not be building on someone else's foundation' (Romans 15:20). The founding of the church in Rome was completely independent of Paul, so it was not his intention to invade their patch or to build on a foundation laid by someone else. His primary function was to evangelize the unevangelized, lay foundations where none yet existed, and consolidate the fruit of his own work through establishing churches and appointing leaders to oversee and direct them, before moving his attention on to new territory and doing the same thing all over again.

Writing towards the end of his third journey as he travelled through Greece on his way back to Jerusalem he said, 'There is no more place for me to work in these regions' (Romans 15:23), not because they had been completely and successfully evangelized, but because Paul had fulfilled the particular work that was his personal priority. So he looked for new areas into which he might move. In the existing territory of his ministry he was leaving behind new believers he had won to Christ, having established them as healthy communities that would serve as a bridgehead to the many still unreached people throughout the area, but it was time for him personally to move on. Their work would continue on and on and never be finished, but his own work as the pioneer evangelist and establisher of churches in the area was concluded.

There were risks of course in this approach, for he lamented to the Corinthians that the builders who worked on his foundation were not always as careful as they could and should have been, resulting in some of the worldly outlook and immature activities he had cause to write to them about: 'I laid a foundation as an expert builder, and someone else is building on it. But each one should be careful how he builds' (1 Corinthians 3:10).

If Paul saw his ministry as going where no one else had gone and laying the foundation for a work of God in a new area, how did he do it? Once there is a nucleus of believers in any given area there is the possibility of a bridgehead into the local community through which Christ may be made known and others 'added to their number' (Acts 2:47). But how do you form the initial nucleus of believers where none exist in the first place? Where do you actually start? What principles of operation should govern pioneer evangelism and missionary outreach? Paul has much to teach us about this.

Building a bridge from known to unknown issues

It is an important principle of communication that we teach what is unknown by means of what is known. Beginning with the familiar, we build a bridge to the unfamiliar. This is the genius of parables where familiar issues are used to teach unfamiliar truths. On a very simple level if, for example, I told you I had in my hand a plastic tube about 7 inches long, with a detachable head, and an inner tube containing a red substance, you may correctly form the idea in your mind that I have a pen in my hand. You will have no real idea as to the precise shape, make, style or colour of the pen, except that it contains red ink. If, however, I were to hold up a black pen in one hand and tell you I have a similar red pen in my other hand, you would know exactly what is in my hand. I have identified the unseen pen with the visible one and told you the one difference is that it has red ink and not black. I have thereby taught you something you did not know by linking it to something you do know.

If our attempts to communicate something new begin with the unfamiliar we will almost certainly confuse those we are trying to instruct, and ultimately leave them as ignorant of what we want them to know as they were in the first place. But if we start with what is already familiar to our hearers and carefully build a bridge from that to the previously unfamiliar truths we wish them to know, we are likely to communicate and take people with us in their understanding. Paul's tactic and skill in preaching was to communicate the truths of the gospel that were unknown to his hearers, by means of things already known to them. He looked for a common platform on which he could begin to construct a bridge that would take his listeners from their own familiar territory into the new territory of the gospel truths he wanted them to know. This meant he worked at becoming as familiar with the world of his hearers as he was with the world of the Scriptures he preached, for he could only communicate the latter in the context of the former. That is why we too need to be as familiar with our newspapers as we are with our Bibles, as aware of our cultural values and expectations as we are with God's truth if we are going to communicate effectively to those outside Christ. Let us look at several examples of Paul's ability to do this.

Jews in their synagogues

When Paul came to a new city he normally sought out the Jewish synagogue, if one existed, as his first point of contact with the people. It was not because he was promoting Judaism or endorsing the ritualism of a system he spent so much of his time repudiating, but because there existed in the synagogue the open Scriptures and a familiarity with the history and rituals of their covenant with God that Paul knew were pointers to Christ.

Jewish synagogues were to be found in most cities around the Mediterranean scenes of Paul's travels, because in the two or three centuries prior to Christ, there had been a voluntary dispersion of Jews throughout the ancient world. Many had earlier been scattered through the enforced exile that followed the Babylonian conquest of Judah, and had chosen not to return to Israel when the Persian conquerors of Babylon permitted many of its exiled peoples to do so. During the later

Greek and Roman eras, however, many Jewish people had chosen to leave their homeland and seek better opportunities elsewhere as merchants, farmers or skilled craftspeople, establishing in many cities their own ethnic communities. We know, for instance, that as many as one million Jews resided in Egypt alone during the first century after Christ, with a similarly large group in Syria immediately to the north of Israel. Many others travelled as far as Italy, and something like 50,000 Jews are known to have been resident in Rome during the first century.

Throughout the Roman Empire during this time the Jews enjoyed the privileges of religious liberty, practising and even propagating their beliefs quite freely. The local synagogue, characteristically referred to as a 'prayer house', became the focal point of each Jewish community.

There was of course only one temple in Judaism where sacrifices and offerings could be made to God through the established priesthood, and that was located in Jerusalem, known as the 'holy city' by virtue of the temple's presence there. Throughout the Jewish homeland and wherever the Jewish people scattered across the Mediterranean world, there were numerous synagogues. These were not only the centres of religious observance, but were the focus of Jewish culture and tradition. Every Jewish community had its synagogue.

The Sabbath was the appointed day for public worship, when all would gather together, along with any 'Gentiles who worship God' (as, for example, in Pisidian Antioch; see Acts 13:16) and in Athens or Corinth where 'God-fearing Greeks' (Acts 17:17; 18:4) also joined them. The latter presumably recognized some satisfying expression of God in Judaism and so joined in Jewish worship, many becoming proselytes. The procedure in synagogue gatherings followed that of an open forum where anyone could volunteer to speak, provided the synagogue ruler considered the person suitable, or where he initiated their participation by inviting them to do so. Paul, as a trained Pharisee, came to the synagogue with strong credentials in his favour, particularly having been a student of Gamaliel. He had the advantage, when he initially arrived in a new city, of the fact that his poor reputation in the Jewish communities had not always preceded him. So here in the synagogue was an open door among people who desired to know and worship God, where the Scriptures were open and accessible, and from which starting point Paul could easily build a bridge to Christ.

Consequently, on his first missionary journey with Barnabas, we find them preaching in the synagogues of Salamis on Cyprus, in Pisidian Antioch and in Iconium, where 'Paul and Barnabas went *as usual* into the Jewish synagogue' (Acts 14:1, my emphasis). This had become their *usual* practice, clearly involving many additional places not specifically named. On Paul's second missionary journey, this time with Silas as his chief companion, he preached in the synagogues of Thessalonica, Berea, Athens, Corinth and briefly Ephesus, before returning there on his third missionary journey and taking up his ministry again in the synagogue, this time preaching to the same crowd every Sabbath day for three months. In every centre they were welcomed and initially encouraged to participate in the synagogue service. Arriving in Pisidian Antioch, 'the synagogue rulers sent word to them, saying, "Brothers, if you have a message of encouragement for the people, please speak"' (Acts 13:15).

The only record we have of what Paul actually preached in the synagogue is a summary of his message in Pisidian Antioch. It makes an interesting study in good communication. He began with a survey of Israel's history, something not only already familiar to his hearers, but which was the foundation of their identity, meaning and purpose as a nation. He is on familiar, secure home territory with them. Addressing them as 'children of Abraham' he begins his story with their dramatic deliverance from Egypt under Moses, the occupation of Canaan, the raising up of Judges to govern the nation, the appointment of the first disastrous king, Saul, and his replacement by David, whom God described as 'a man after my own heart'. So far, there is nothing controversial, nothing out of the ordinary and no paradigm shift required on the part of his hearers. They are probably nodding in agreement, impressed with his grasp of the subject and secure in the familiar territory along which he is taking them. This is wise, good, wholesome communication. So far so good. But Paul now has to build a bridge from the familiar things about which he has been talking to the unfamiliar things he wants them to know.

If the history and traditions of Judaism form one side of a chasm that separates Paul's hearers from the gospel of Jesus Christ, having dug deep foundations in that territory, he must now build a bridge across the chasm to the other side he wants them to know. The unfamiliar message he is about to present has to come to them with roots in familiar terms if it is to be understood. Paul skilfully does this by talking about the descendants of Israel's greatest and most revered king, David, whose line was destined to occupy the throne of Israel for ever. In this context he makes his first introduction of Christ when he says, 'From this man's descendants God has brought to Israel the Saviour Jesus, as he promised' (Acts 13:23). His focus is still 'to Israel', for to speak of Gentile inclusion at this stage would be to step out of the familiar territory of his Jewish hearers and present too big a stumbling block for them to cross, giving them a legitimate justification in their own thinking to reject his message (something he later experienced in Jerusalem where his mention of being sent to the Gentiles provoked such a hostile response that they declared him not fit to live – see Acts 22:22). Having built his bridge from the familiar territory of the Old Testament revelation to his main message, the person and significance of Christ, Paul then affirms to his hearers, 'It is to us that this message of salvation has been sent' and he moves on to more detail of the life and ministry of Christ, his rejection by his own people, his death and resurrection from the dead and how these events were actually foreseen and prophesied in the Scriptures that are opened and read in the synagogues each week. Paul then explains the implications of this, the need for repentance, and the possibility of forgiveness of sin.

Such was the response to the clarity and sense of this that the next Sabbath, 'almost the whole city gathered to hear the word of the Lord'. But it did not take very long before reaction set in when some Jews 'talked abusively against what Paul was saying' (Acts 13:45), and very soon they 'stirred up persecution against Paul and Barnabas, and expelled them from their region' (Acts 13:50). But this inevitable opposition, a pattern that consistently followed Paul wherever he went, was set against a minority who had listened, understood and responded to his message and become believers in the Lord Jesus Christ, so that as Luke reports from Pisidian Antioch at the time of this event, 'all who were appointed for eternal life believed' (Acts 13:48).

The thinking of Paul was that in the synagogues there would be found those who, by their presence, were evidently open to God and concerned to worship him. There were of course many for whom the rituals of Judaism had replaced the reality of knowing God, to whom form had become more important than substance, and for whom Paul was a threat and a mischief-maker who needed to be silenced. But when those whose hearts God was opening heard, on their own territory, a message not completely alien, but that grew out of the soil of their own previous knowledge and assumptions, they understood and were able to respond.

But what about places where there was no synagogue? Paul also adopted a similar approach on those occasions by seeking out any interest in knowing, seeking or worshipping God, and at whatever point he found that, whether it be in idolatry or something closer to a desire to know the real God, he would familiarize himself with their territory, identify with it, and from that position build a bridge to God.

Women in Philippi

When Paul arrived in Philippi for the first time, Luke was one of his travelling companions and he reports that on the Sabbath 'we went outside the city gate to the river, where we expected to find a place of prayer' (Acts 16:13). There was evidently no synagogue in Philippi, presumably because there were few Jewish men living there. It required a quorum of ten Jewish men to establish a synagogue, and no number of women would make up for the absence of even just one man of the ten minimum.[1] There was however a 'place of prayer', attended entirely by women and which met outside the city on the Sabbath day. We don't know the nature of this prayer group, or who they understood themselves to be praying to, though it was probably a small group of Jewish ladies, indicated by the fact that they met on the Sabbath, but who were denied the more formal meetings a synagogue in their city would have provided for them.

Paul and his companions joined themselves to this group, sat down with the women and began to talk. We don't know the substance of what they said, except that they explained the gospel to them and as a result a lady named Lydia who is described as a 'worshipper of God' was intrigued by what she heard, and 'The Lord opened her heart to respond to Paul's message' (Acts 16:14). Paul didn't criticize their praying to a

---

[1] See F.F. Bruce, *The Book of Acts* (Marshall, Morgan and Scott, 1972), p. 331.

God they didn't know, or try to correct a faulty understanding by which they may have hoped to gain access to God, though we may be sure these beliefs were inconsistent with the gospel Paul preached. Instead, recognizing the disposition of their hearts as women seeking God, he gave them a positive message that centred on Jesus Christ. The result of this was that as they understood and embraced the truth, they responded to Paul's message.

It is a far better tactic to offer truth positively to people than to try to destroy what they hold dear and what we may recognize as their faulty understanding. If you try to take a bone away from the mouth of a hungry dog, the dog will attack you and probably tear you to pieces. But if you put a piece of steak on the ground, the dog will soon leave the bone and pick up the steak. Paul's strategy was not to take the bone from the mouth of the dog, provoking a defensiveness that would probably soon turn to anger on the part of those he wanted to help, but to lay down the steak, presenting the positive message of the fullness of life to be found in Jesus Christ, with little or no reference to their current misbelief. Like Lydia, people soon find their hearts opened by the Holy Spirit, and in the course of time will begin to leave the 'bones' behind on their own initiative as they discover and enjoy the new 'steak' of the rich life they have found in Christ.

Out of that little prayer meeting for women beside the river, Paul built a bridge from their current understanding of things to the full message of life in Jesus Christ, and as one and another of the women responded, the church in Philippi was born.

Pagans in Lystra

What about where there is neither synagogue nor place of prayer? How do we build a bridge to those not actively seeking for God in any obvious way at all? On Paul's visit to Lystra during his first missionary journey, he encountered in the midst of a crowd a man crippled in both feet, but who 'had faith to be healed' (Acts 14:9). Recognizing this, Paul commanded, 'Stand up on your feet!' and immediately the man jumped up and began to walk. Such was the stunning impact of this event on the crowd, that they began shouting, 'The gods have come down to us in human form!' and they prostrated themselves before Paul and Barnabas, sent for the priest of Zeus from a pagan temple outside the city to bring bulls and wreaths, and prepared to offer sacrifices to the apostles. Barnabas they called by the name of Zeus, and Paul they called Hermes. According to an ancient local legend, Zeus (known in Latin as Jupiter) was the chief god and as Barnabas was the leader of the two men, he was called Zeus. Hermes (known in Latin as Mercury) was his son, the herald and preacher of the gods, which is why they attributed this title to Paul, who by this time had become the main speaker.

Needless to say, Paul and Barnabas were stunned by this response, at first unable to understand what was going on because the people were shouting in the Lycaonian language which they didn't know. When they realized they had become objects of worship they tore their clothes, a gesture among Jews of horror at blasphemy, and rushed into the crowd shouting, 'We too are only men, human like you' (Acts 14:15). Having fully got the attention of this crowd of pagan idolaters, the challenge next facing Paul was to build a bridge from their presuppositions and superstitions to Jesus Christ. And he did so magnificently. To compare his preaching here with his preaching in the synagogue is to find a complete contrast of substance, but complete unanimity of purpose. In the synagogue his text was the open Scriptures of the Old Testament with which his listeners were familiar. His audience in Lystra were not Jews, but pagans, schooled only by the priests of Zeus in their legends, superstitions and idolatry, and completely ignorant of the Old Testament, so Paul made no reference to it at all. Instead he began with the only Bible they had – the revelation of God in creation around and above them:

> We are bringing you good news, telling you to turn from these worthless things to the living God, who made heaven and earth and sea and everything in them. In the past, he let all nations go their own way. Yet he has not left himself without testimony: He has shown kindness by giving you rain from heaven and crops in their seasons; he provides you with plenty of food and fills your hearts with joy. (Acts 14:15–17)

Paul explains in his letter to the Romans that God has reliably revealed himself to all people in the very existence of the creation:

> . . . since what may be known about God is plain to them, because God has made it plain to them. For since the creation of the world God's invisible qualities – his eternal power and divine nature – have been clearly seen, being understood from what has been made, so that men are without excuse. (Romans 1:19–20)

A revelation of God can be read across the stars of the night sky, and in the intricacies of a petal on a flower. Long before, David had declared this:

> The heavens declare the glory of God;
>   the skies proclaim the work of his hands.
> Day after day they pour forth speech;
>   night after night they display knowledge.
> There is no speech or language
>   where their voice is not heard.
> Their voice goes out into all the earth,
>   their words to the ends of the world. (Psalm 19:1–4)

Paul appeals to this natural revelation of God in Lystra, extending it beyond God's initial act of creation, to his providing seasons of rain and sunshine, enabling crops to grow and putting food on their tables and joy in their hearts. This is common ground with the people he is addressing. The worship of most pagan deities involved acknowledgements of the basic ingredients to sustain life. Paul recognized this and established it as common ground from which to build a bridge from their worldview to Christ.

The attention of the narrative is then diverted from the conclusion of Paul's message to the fact that some Jews came from Antioch and Iconium to persuade the crowd that Paul and Barnabas were just a couple of troublemakers, stirring people up wherever they went, and should be seen off at once. The crowd were won over, and from one moment when 'they had difficulty keeping the crowd from sacrificing to them' (Acts 14:18) their effort turned from attempts to worship the two men to becoming sadistically violent towards them. So much so that 'they stoned Paul and dragged him outside the city, thinking he was dead' (Acts 14:19).

Philosophers in Athens

On his second missionary journey Paul came for the first time to the city of Athens, the world centre for philosophical discourse and debate. Most of the great thinkers of the era spent time here, and Paul found a group of Epicurean and Stoic philosophers ready to enjoy some intellectual sparring with him. Luke tells us rather disparagingly, 'All the Athenians and the foreigners who lived there spent their time doing nothing but talking about and listening to the latest ideas' (Acts 17:21).

Paul followed his custom in Athens of first seeking out the Jewish community and preaching in their synagogues, but he also went beyond the Jews into the market place day by day to reason and debate with those who were willing to listen and participate. One day he was brought to a meeting of the Areopagus – the highly respected aristocratic court of Athens which, although it had lost much of its original power at the time of Paul, still exercised some jurisdiction over religious and ethical matters. Paul was brought before this court to give an account of his message and philosophy. Once again he took the opportunity to build a bridge to Christ by starting from where they were in their thinking and philosophy.

The inscription he has seen on a pagan altar amid the many objects of worship in the city, 'TO AN UNKNOWN GOD', becomes his text. If there is a God at all, most of the philosophers of Athens held the consensus that he was unknown and probably unknowable. Once again, he is out of the synagogue among people unfamiliar with Jewish history, so any appeal he might make to the Old Testament Scriptures would be completely meaningless and not only lost on his hearers but presenting a significant barrier to them. Instead, as in Lystra earlier, he refers to the revelation that leaves all men 'without excuse' (Romans 1:20), the existence of creation:

> The God who made the world and everything in it is the Lord of heaven and earth and does not live in temples built by hands. And he is not served by human hands, as if he needed anything, because he himself gives all men life and breath and everything else. From one man he made every nation of men, that they should inhabit the whole earth; and he determined the times set for them and the exact places where they should live. God did this so that men would seek him and perhaps reach out for him and find him, though he is not far from each one of us. 'For in him we live and move and have our being.' As some of your own poets have said, 'We are his offspring.'
>
> Therefore since we are God's offspring, we should not think that the divine being is like gold or silver or stone – an image made by man's design and skill. In the past God overlooked such ignorance,

but now he commands all people everywhere to repent. For he has set a day when he will judge the world with justice by the man he has appointed. He has given proof of this to all men by raising him from the dead. (Acts 17:24–31)

Beginning with acknowledgement of the dilemma of an 'Unknown God', Paul again appeals to the evidence of his existence in creation. He quotes the poets and philosophers of Athens to establish a sense of the need for dependency on God, refers to the futile attempts of men to express God in terms of gold, silver and stone images scattered around the area where he is speaking, and then brings them to the fact that God has been willing to overlook 'such ignorance' but now things have changed. Paul has skilfully led them across the bridge from the known and familiar to what had been until now unfamiliar to his hearers: the work of Christ and his resurrection from the dead.

It was his statement about the resurrection of the dead that provoked a sneering response from the philosophers for whom anything supernatural was discounted. Paul, however, had built his bridge to Christ. He had not only given a logical, intelligent means of crossing to a new understanding of life, but the means by which the Holy Spirit could bear witness to the truth in the hearts of some who heard, so that 'A few men became followers of Paul and believed' (Acts 17:34). This included people of sufficient renown to cause Luke to name them: Dionysius a member of the Areopagus and thereby distinguished among the people of Athens (and possibly, as one tradition affirms, later to become first Bishop of Athens), and a woman named Damaris about whom we know nothing other than the fact that Luke by naming her indicates she was a woman of some prominence.

Paul was a master communicator. His audience did not determine the ultimate content of his message for, as he explained to the Corinthians, whose city he visited for the first time immediately after this visit to Athens, 'I resolved to know nothing while I was with you except Jesus Christ and him crucified' (1 Corinthians 2:2). But his audience did shape the means by which he presented that message. Paul's starting point was always as far back as it needed to be in the thinking, culture and presuppositions of his hearers, for without first getting onto their territory and into their minds he could not have taken them anywhere else. Once he had found his starting point in some common ground between his hearers and his message, however, his destination was always the same: the proclamation of the life, death and resurrection of Jesus Christ and the possibility of life that derives from repentance towards God and faith in Jesus Christ.

8

Restoring Righteousness

Paul was primarily and essentially an evangelist. The word 'evangelist' only occurs three times in the New Testament: twice by Paul, first in his list of the gifts of the risen Christ to his church (Ephesians 4:11), and secondly when in his closing years he encouraged Timothy in Ephesus to 'do the work of an evangelist' (2 Timothy 4:5). The other occasion is in the book of Acts as a description of Philip (Acts 21:8), one of the seven men initially set apart to serve the practical interests of the church in Jerusalem, but who subsequently became a prominent preacher after the martyrdom of Stephen.

The word 'evangelist' is the noun from the verb meaning 'to announce news'. In one sense, every Christian is to be an evangelist because it is the intention of the Lord Jesus Christ that all of his people are involved in evangelism, announcing the good news to others. Immediately after the martyrdom of Stephen the church in Jerusalem was scattered throughout Judea, Samaria and further afield, not only to escape the persecution brewing in Jerusalem but as an opportunity for the dispersing church to evangelize. Luke tells us that 'those who had been scattered preached the word wherever they went' (Acts 8:4). One paraphrase states they 'gossiped the gospel'. Christians naturally and spontaneously talked about the good news to whomever they met, whenever they met and wherever they met. This was not a programme organized and led by the apostles in Jerusalem, but a spontaneous expression of the newly discovered life these ordinary people had found in Christ.

Important as it is, however, to recognize the general responsibility God has given to all Christians, God gives the specific gifts and abilities of the evangelist to some in particular. Paul was supremely one of these. He was not a 'church planter' (there is no such classification in the New Testament); he was an evangelist. Church planting seems to be supremely concerned with strategies and tactics, whereas evangelism is concerned supremely with people! The consequence of Paul's evangelism was that churches were founded, but the establishing of churches was the inevitable fruit of his ministry, not the goal. The goal was reconciling people to God.

In considering the role of the evangelist, it is important to ask the question 'What is the message of the evangelist?' What exactly is the 'good news' that revolutionized countless lives throughout the Mediterranean world in Paul's day, and has continued to revolutionize lives ever since? Fortunately, we don't have to piece together Paul's gospel from fragments of his messages scattered around the New Testament, for Paul took time to spell out his message clearly in his letter to the Romans, which has often rightly been called a Christian manifesto.[1]

Paul had never been to Rome, but he wrote to the church there as he drew to the close of his third missionary journey, to let them know that his future plans included fulfilling an ambition to take the gospel to Spain. En route to this most westerly peninsula in southern Europe, he hoped to call on the

---

[1] See, for example, the 'Preliminary Essay' in John R.W. Stott, *The Message of Romans* (IVP, 1994).

Christians in Rome, not to encroach on their territory, but to provide an opportunity for mutual encouragement. He was aware, however, that this self-invitation to Rome would not be welcomed by everyone, as there continued to be various non-flattering rumours circulating that made some Christians wary and suspicious of him. In order to counter any misapprehensions about him, he set out to explain the substance of his message and the gospel he would preach if he were to come to them. The resulting letter to the Romans is Paul's most systematic presentation of his message, and as such is the clearest explanation of what the gospel actually is.

In this sense Romans is unique. Most of Paul's other letters are motivated by a pastoral concern for a group of people he has been personally involved with, in most cases having been instrumental in leading them to Christ and establishing them as a church, so he is writing to answer specific questions they have sent him, or he is correcting their doctrines, or reprimanding their behaviour. The only letter apart from Romans that Paul wrote to a church he had not yet visited was his letter to the Colossians. Here he took the opportunity of writing while sending Onesimus, a runaway slave whom he had met in prison and led to Christ, back to Philemon, his Christian owner in Colosse.[2] Word had reached Paul of some encouraging things in Colosse but also of the disturbing news that false teaching had infiltrated the church and was threatening to lead the people away from the truth of Christ. So he took the opportunity of correcting this error while communicating with Colosse. But his letter to the Romans addresses no problem, corrects no error and reprimands no behaviour. Rather, it comes down to us as the fullest and most systematic affirmation of the gospel we have in the New Testament.

---

[2] See the letter to Philemon.

Paul summarizes the gospel early in the letter when he explains:

> That is why I am so eager to preach the gospel also to you who are at Rome. I am not ashamed of the gospel, because it is the power of God for the salvation of everyone who believes: first for the Jew, then for the Gentile. (Romans 1:15–16)

It is easy at that point to read into the statement some preconceived idea of what he means by the 'gospel' and what the 'power of God' is for. But we do not need to do that, for Paul continues, 'For in the gospel a righteousness from God is revealed, a righteousness that is by faith from first to last, just as it is written: "The righteous will live by faith"' (Romans 1:17). What he is saying is that the gospel is about the righteousness of God, not simply as an objective truth about God, but as something made available to us, 'a righteousness *from* God' and obtainable 'by faith'.

Salvation therefore, according to Paul, is not primarily a salvation from guilt to innocence, or from hell to heaven, or even from death to life (each of which reflects so many popular views but only deals with subsidiary issues). Salvation is primarily *from unrighteousness to righteousness*. It is true that the *cause* of this is that we are forgiven and made clean. It is true its *consequence* is that we will go to heaven and not to hell. It is true that the *means* to this end is by being made alive through the gift of the Holy Spirit who imparts spiritual life to us. But salvation encompasses something far bigger and more significant than each of those issues. It is a *salvation from unrighteousness to righteousness*. Significantly, Paul never once mentions heaven as the goal of the Christian life in either Romans or in any other of his letters (nor, incidentally, does Jesus). Paul's only two references to heaven in Romans relate to 'The wrath of God . . .

being revealed from heaven' (Romans 1:18) and 'Do not say in your heart, "Who will ascend into heaven?" (that is, to bring Christ down)' (Romans 10:6). Heaven is real, and a wonderful consequence of the gospel to which we may confidently and eagerly look forward, but inhabiting heaven is not the purpose of the gospel.

Christ did not come into the world to recruit for heaven, but to reconcile humanity to God so that God's purposes in creating us might be restored and fulfilled. The work of Jesus was not to commence something completely new but to mend the broken state of humanity and restore us to our original purpose. If your car is broken down on the side of the road, your prime concern will not be whether you have a garage at home to put it in when you eventually get there, but to fix the car so that it will function properly and take you down the road. That is the purpose of the car! Once you get the car started and are able to drive it down the road, having a garage in which to put it may be important and valuable – but you don't mend the car for the purpose of being able to put it in the garage! You mend it in order to be able to drive it along the road – as was the manufacturer's intention.

The restoring of the righteousness of God into human experience is mending broken humanity that lies on the side of the road, unable to fulfil the purpose for which we were created. Jesus came to put back into human experience the life of God that Adam had lost in the Garden of Eden. God had declared to Adam, 'You must not eat from the tree of the knowledge of good and evil, for when you eat of it you will surely die' (Genesis 2:17). Some translations state specifically, 'In the day you eat thereof you shall die.' In what sense did Adam die on the day he ate of the fruit? It was not physically, for he lived many more years, but he endured spiritual death. In the words of Paul he became 'separated from the life of God' (Ephesians

4:18). Paul's gospel begins with the presupposition that this is
the state into which every human being since Adam (with the
sole exception of Christ) is born, for 'in Adam all die'
(1 Corinthians 15:22), and in consequence every human being
is by nature unable to be the visible expression of the moral
image of God, which was God's original purpose for humanity.
Instead of expressing the righteousness of God in our behaviour, we are universally in the sorry state of 'There is no-one
righteous, not even one' (Romans 3:10).

The righteousness of God is in the first instance a description
of his moral character. *The Concise Oxford Dictionary* defines
the word as applying to that which is 'morally right; virtuous;
law abiding'. In the beginning, the Scriptures tell us, God created
mankind in his own image (Genesis 1:26). Christian theologians
have long debated the precise nature of the image of God in
humanity, and will continue to do so, but essentially the image
is a moral one. There are what we may describe as the *incommunicable* attributes of God (that is, they are uniquely his and
cannot be imparted to, or shared by, anyone else) and there are
the *communicable* attributes (that is, they may be imparted to, or
shared by, another). God's incommunicable attributes include
his omnipotence (he is all-powerful), his omniscience (he is all-
knowing), his omnipresence (he is in all places at all times), his
immutability (he is unchanging with time), and his eternal being
(he has neither a beginning nor an end). These qualities belong
uniquely to God and are not shared by any part of his creation.
But the communicable attributes of God are those that belong
to his moral character, such as his righteousness, his justice and
his love. It is these qualities that the gospel centres on restoring,
for it is these qualities that were lost in the Fall.

If the ultimate goal of Paul's gospel is restoring the righteousness of God into human experience, then it follows we can only
understand what this is if we first understand the righteousness

of God himself. Paul uses the words 'righteous' and 'righteous-ness' more than 100 times in his letters, indicating the central place this theme has in his gospel. It carries both objective and subjective connotations. Objectively we are *made righteous* (Romans 5:19), meaning that in our standing before God we are justified – a legal position that frees us from condemnation. This is not something we deserve, but is made possible only by the work of Jesus Christ in addressing the wrath of God through his death as a substitute for the guilty. This is Paul's most frequent use of the term.

If, however, as far as our position before God is concerned, our righteousness is an accomplished act, there is also a subjective and continuing element to righteousness, for Paul tells us to 'offer the parts of your body to him as instruments of right-eousness' (Romans 6:13). This is the ongoing process in which our standing before God is expressed in our submission to God and our consequent behaviour before the world. This is why the 'fruit of the Spirit is love, joy, peace, patience, kindness, good-ness, faithfulness, gentleness and self-control' (Galatians 5:22–23), all of which are moral qualities, and the inevitable expression of the Holy Spirit's presence and activity in people.

As Paul states, 'In the gospel a righteousness from God is revealed, a righteousness that is by faith.' It follows that before there is any real interest in the righteousness of God on our part there must correspondingly be an awareness of our own unrighteousness. People do not become aware of sin (their unrighteousness) by simply being told about sin. That will prob-ably only get their backs up! They become aware of sin by becoming aware of God's moral character, against which they see themselves to have fallen short. Sin, by Paul's definition, is 'coming short of the glory of God' (Romans 3:23). It is literally missing a mark (the word was used in archery to describe an arrow that missed its target). If someone were playing with a bow and arrow in a field, they might enjoy the exhilaration of the tension of the bow as they pull back the arrow and release it into the distance. It might be great fun and keep them occupied for hours. But if someone came into the field and put up a target and challenged them to aim for and hit the target, the feelings of exhilaration might subside fairly quickly as their incompetence becomes painfully apparent. That is why the first task of the evangelist is not to preach sin, but to preach Christ. The awareness of Christ *leads* to an awareness of sin, such as was evident when Peter preached on the Day of Pentecost, and told the story of Jesus without making any mention of the personal sin of his hearers. Suddenly the crowd asked, 'What shall we do?' to which Peter was then able to reply, 'Repent' (Acts 2:37–38). Similarly, Paul states that it is our knowledge of God's righteousness that makes us aware of sin, for 'through the law we become conscious of sin' (Romans 3:20). He also writes, 'So then, the law is holy, and the commandment is holy, righteous and good' (Romans 7:12), for the law in this context reveals, and is equal to, the righteousness of God. In other words, the law in its moral demands represents everything God is in his moral character. That is why Paul also writes of 'the righteous requirements of the law' (Romans 8:4), indicating that the righteousness of God is expressed in the demands of the law.

If, on the one hand, the righteousness of God exposes the unrighteousness of humanity, on the other hand, Paul states that an awareness of our own unrighteousness enhances our knowledge of God's righteousness, for 'our unrighteousness brings out God's righteousness more clearly' (Romans 3:5). We will therefore not have an understanding of our own unrighteousness without knowing God's righteousness, and we cannot understand God's righteousness without an awareness of our own failure. That is why the starting point in Paul's gospel is that an awareness of our sin derives from an awareness of the righteous demands of the law, for it is 'through the law we become conscious of sin' (Romans 3:20). An emphasis on the grace of God is legitimate, meaningful and necessary only in the context of an understanding of the law of God, for we can only appreciate grace when we know how far short we have fallen and how absolutely helpless we are to do anything about it ourselves. It is then that the kindness of God becomes marvellous good news to us, not just in getting us 'off the hook' and easing our conscience so that we no longer stand guilty before God, but in equipping us to live holy, purposeful and fruitful lives.

Law and grace are not two conflicting issues in Paul's writings, with the law belonging to the old redundant covenant, and grace to the new. Our appreciation and experience of the grace of God grows out of an awareness of our own bankruptcy and sin, which derives in turn only from understanding the demands of God's law. If we do not know the demands of God's law we can sin with a clear conscience, as Paul affirms, 'I would not have known what sin was except through the law' (Romans 7:7). A policeman cannot make a speeding driver aware of his error simply by pointing to his speedometer – the driver must also be aware of the speed limit on the road. It is only when the driver is aware that the limit is 50 mph that the policeman can meaningfully tell him that as his speed was 70 mph he is in trouble.

On what grounds may we tell a person that to lie, to cheat, to commit adultery or to be greedy is wrong? People do not know what sin is because they do not know who God is, and they do not know who God is because they do not know his law. This is why the first requirement of the gospel is an understanding of the law. This is exactly Paul's message to the Romans, where he explains at the outset the revelation of God in creation then through the law, leading to a conclusion for which the law has given irrefutable evidence: 'There is no-one righteous, not even one' (Romans 3:10). Until we have understood this truth we are not able to appreciate or experience the grace of God.

Grace grows out of law; it does not substitute for law. In the light of the requirements of the law, demands no human being can meet, Paul explains:

> But now a righteousness from God, apart from law, has been made known, to which the Law and the Prophets testify. This righteousness from God comes through faith in Jesus Christ to all who believe. (Romans 3:21–22)

This is where the grace of God comes into play because 'where sin increased, grace increased all the more' (Romans 5:20). The greater our consciousness of our sin, the greater our enjoyment of grace. This is why Paul writes, 'The law was added so that the trespass might increase,' not so that we might be humiliated and condemned through an increasing exposure to our own trespass, but that we might exchange our guilt for a righteousness we do not deserve and cannot earn, but are invited to receive. Grace is God giving us what we don't deserve. Grace is not God saying our sin doesn't matter any more, for it matters deeply, but that having met the demand of our sin in the cross, Christ himself may now administer cleansing and restoration enabling us to live on the basis of his grace.

If the goal of the gospel is restoring the righteousness of God to human experience, then the means by which that is accomplished is through the imparting of the life of God to the believer. Paul told the Romans:

> And if anyone does not have the Spirit of Christ, he does not belong to Christ. But if Christ is in you, your body is dead because of sin, yet your spirit is alive because of righteousness. And if the Spirit of him who raised Jesus from the dead is living in you, he who raised

Christ from the dead will also give life to your mortal bodies through his Spirit, who lives in you. (Romans 8:9–11)

Righteousness is the result of the life of Christ being in us. This is the new birth. It is not God giving us life in some detached form, but God giving us himself. For God to give us himself, our sin needs to be cleansed, which is why the starting point of the Christian life involves confession of sin and repentance. We need to be forgiven of our sin in order to receive the life of God, and we are to receive the life of God in order to express the righteousness of God.

Living by faith

If restoring the righteousness of God to human experience is the goal of the gospel, then how is that possible? Paul answers, 'This righteousness from God comes through faith in Jesus Christ to all who believe' (Romans 3:22). It is on the basis of faith that the righteousness of God is received and experienced. Paul uses the word 'faith' or 'believe' more than 50 times in Romans. In fact, he uses the word 'faith' 142 times in all of his letters, whereas it occurs only 101 times in the rest of the New Testament altogether. So Paul's emphasis on faith can hardly be denied! Faith is the fundamental response we make to God.

Faith as objective

Paul uses the word 'faith' both objectively and subjectively. Objectively, he speaks of 'the faith' as, for example, when he asks the Corinthians to 'Examine yourselves to see whether you are in *the faith;* test yourselves. Do you not realize that Christ Jesus is in you – unless, of course, you fail the test?' (2 Corinthians 13:5, my emphasis); or he exhorts them to 'stand firm in the faith' (1 Corinthians 16:13); and the Philippians are urged to contend 'for *the faith* of the gospel without being frightened in any way by those who oppose you' (Philippians 1:27–28, my emphasis). All these references to 'the faith' are to the body of teaching that is the substance of the Christian message Paul preached from his earliest days, as, for example, when the early believers in Judea 'heard the report: "The man who formerly persecuted us is now preaching *the faith* he once tried to destroy"' (Galatians 1:23).

Faith as subjective

But more frequently, 'faith' is a subjective word in Paul's writing, speaking of the disposition of trust towards God that is the indispensable ingredient both to becoming a Christian and then to living the Christian life. He writes to the Ephesians, 'For it is by grace you have been saved, through faith' (chapter 2:8) – the only grounds on which a person may become a Christian.

But this is not a once-for-all event, so that once we are saved we live from then on by human efforts. He speaks of Christ dwelling in the hearts of believers 'through faith' (Ephesians 3:17), which points to an ongoing activity. We are to 'live by faith' (2 Corinthians 5:7), as a daily disposition of trust in God and obedience to him. Paul looks for growth in faith, saying to the Corinthians, 'Our hope is that, as your faith continues to grow, our area of activity among you will greatly expand' (2 Corinthians 10:15); and to the Thessalonians, 'We ought always to thank God for you, brothers, and rightly so, because your faith is growing more and more, and the love every one of you has for each other is increasing' (2 Thessalonians 1:3). Faith, in Christian experience, is not only a continual event but a growing one.

So what is faith? Some see it as a kind of mystical power, where the act of believing actually makes something happen: if you believe something strongly enough, you may be the cause of its becoming true! But this is not faith. Faith is essentially a disposition of trust towards God that allows God to act. Faith has to be placed in something or someone. We cannot just have 'faith' any more than we can just 'love'. If you are in love at all it must be with somebody. So it is with faith. Faith must be *in* something, and it is the object in which our faith is placed that determines the validity of the faith. If I put my faith in a car, I'm allowing the car to take me down the road. If the car is a battered old wreck, no amount of faith will make up for the deficiency of the car. My faith won't *improve* the car in any way, nor will my lack of faith contribute to its deficiencies: all my faith in the car will do is let the car perform within the capability that it has. Very simply, faith in God is a disposition of trust towards God that allows him to be God in our experience, with all the restrictions on the one hand, and all the possibilities on the other that he may place on his own activity.

Righteousness is by faith for the simple reason that God alone is righteous. So righteousness is only possible as it has its origin in God's presence and activity within us. Left to ourselves, we have to face the reality that 'there is no-one righteous, not even one' (Romans 3:10). When we do attempt to produce our own brand of righteousness that is human in origin, we discover God's verdict on it: 'all our righteous acts are like filthy rags' (Isaiah 64:6). We have nowhere to go for righteousness but to God. We have no power for holy living but from God. So faith is adopting a disposition towards God that allows him to be what he is in us – and he is righteous. The righteousness of God is not only seen in our legal standing before him, but as an ongoing expression of the presence of God within us, shown in our ethical conduct. Paul says to the Galatians, 'For in Christ Jesus neither circumcision nor uncircumcision has any value. The only thing that counts is faith expressing itself through love' (Galatians 5:6). Faith will express itself through love because 'God is love' (1 John 4:8) and the righteousness of God is the moral character of God. We cannot live in dependency on God and not love people, for our failure to love is the extent to which we are quenching the Spirit of God (who is love) within us.

Faith and obedience

If to live by faith is one of Paul's major concerns, then we must not think of faith as merely a passive stance that awaits God's working but is itself inactive. Writing to the Romans Paul talks about 'the obedience that comes from faith' (Romans 1:5). Faith in God involves active obedience. The consequence of putting our faith in God is that we become characterized by obedience to God, and actively pursue his will, not begrudgingly, as though it is the awful price we have to pay for our salvation, but inevitably. Obedience is not something additional to faith, but is the natural and inevitable expression of true faith for those who genuinely trust Christ and are obedient to his will. To obey is part of what it means to trust. It is not that we will be doing things *for* God so much as that God will be doing things *in*, *for* and *through* us, so that his character and his purposes become evident in us. That is why we cannot separate obedience from faith. Obedience without a corresponding trust in God will lead to legalism. Faith without a corresponding obedience will lead to mysticism. They are like the two wings of an aeroplane. Which wing would you suppose to be more important? Each is mutually dependent on the other!

This is the heart of Paul's message and the criterion by which all the practical instruction of his epistles is controlled. To Paul, the ultimate goal of God in human experience is the establishing of his righteousness, the expression of God's character in human experience, on the basis of faith in and obedience to Christ.

9

Facing Foolish Christians

I am convinced that we preachers often preach to our personal weaknesses. It is usually the areas where we have experienced most deeply the liberating grace of God in place of our own deficiencies that we feel most confident to speak passionately about to others. Paul's background as a Pharisee had been one of the strictest legalism. He claimed to the Philippian church, 'As for legalistic righteousness, [I was] faultless' (Philippians 3:6). That was some claim! Having made that claim, however, he went on to relinquish it: 'But whatever was to my profit I consider loss for the sake of Christ' (Philippians 3:7). Paul's legalism, his passionate and fairly successful attempt to keep the law, was the expression of his desire to please God. Having made the discovery on the Damascus road, however, that God's requirements can never be met by human activity alone, but by divine action worked out through human experience, there was nothing consequently that irritated the apostle more than to see believers reverting to Christian living based on human effort, rather than on the presence and working of the Holy Spirit within them.

Returning to Antioch from his first missionary journey, Paul discovered that some Jewish converts to Christianity had come from Jerusalem and were teaching, 'Unless you are circumcised, according to the custom taught by Moses, you cannot be saved' (Acts 15:1). What they were really saying was that if you want to become a Christian you have first to become a Jew. The rationale for this is not hard to understand. Christianity is not unrelated to Judaism for it is in fact the fulfilment and completion of all that the Jewish laws and rituals represented and pointed to. To early Jewish converts, it had come as a wonderful, life-transforming discovery that all the symbolism and rituals of the Old Covenant with which they were so familiar, and which moulded the pattern of their lives, were not just an end in themselves, but pointed clearly to Jesus Christ and found their true fulfilment in his person and work. On understanding this they embraced Christ and became believers in him. Then, however, they had the difficult problem of going back over all that had legitimately characterized their religious observances before they had come to know Christ, and working out how to relate their new relationship to Christ to the God-given laws of Moses that belonged to the Old Covenant. Many of them found no convincing reason why these laws should be dropped.

The act of circumcision, over which the issue erupted in Antioch itself, was only the tip of the iceberg, for it represented the whole of the law of Moses. Circumcision was the covenant sign for the chosen people of God, given to Abraham as an 'everlasting covenant' when he was promised that a nation would come from his own body. To refuse that sign would result in being cut off from the people of God (Genesis 17:9–14). The fact that circumcision was described by God as an 'everlasting covenant' probably contributed to the Judaizers' conviction that this remained an indispensable ingredient in their relationship with God, and thus their conclusion that 'unless you are circumcised according to the law of Moses you cannot be saved'. The 'everlasting' dimension to the covenant with

Abraham was to be ongoing only through its fulfilment in Christ, for from its inception, his coming was its purpose and goal. Paul defines a Jew under the New Covenant not through outward, physical circumcision, but 'circumcision of the heart, by the Spirit, not by the written code' (Romans 2:28–29).

However, the argument presented by the contingent from Jerusalem to the church in Antioch clearly had substance, for it was so convincing that men of such stature and understanding as the apostle Peter, who was spending time in Antioch, were convinced by their argument, and Paul's close companion and friend, Barnabas, freshly back from his first missionary journey with Paul, was also persuaded and 'led astray' by the arguments. This indicates it was no light matter, nor were the issues as clear to the Jews then as they are to Gentiles reading the Scriptures today, separated by time, distance and the Jewish context of these first converts (see Galatians 2:11–13).

Not only did many of the church in Antioch respond positively to this teaching on circumcision, but these Judaizers then followed the trail of Paul's first missionary journey to impress upon his converts their need to be circumcised too, if they were to be sure of their salvation. This active propagation provoked Paul's letter to the Galatians, Galatia being the area in which his first missionary journey had largely taken place,[1] and where he was particularly protective of his converts against these preachers of a 'different gospel' who were 'throwing you into confusion and . . . trying to pervert the gospel of Christ' (Galatians 1:7).

---

[1] There are two possible locations for the territory known as Galatia. Some argue for it being in northern Asia Minor, and others for it being in southern Asia Minor, including the towns of Pisidian Antioch, Iconium, Lystra and Derbe visited by Paul and Barnabas on their first journey (Acts 13 – 14). We are here accepting the southern location favoured by F.F. Bruce and a number of other Pauline scholars.

This issue of the place of the law in Christian discipleship was not easily resolved, and continued to raise its head throughout the New Testament period. Paul warned the Philippian church many years later to 'watch out for those dogs, those men who do evil, those mutilators of the flesh' (Philippians 3:2) who were encouraging circumcision in a town where there had evidently been no synagogue and therefore few Jewish people. Yet this church had become infiltrated by those who chose to insist on the circumcision of Gentile believers as a necessary means to pleasing God.

The Jerusalem Council

To resolve the conflict in Antioch, a meeting was arranged in Jerusalem between Paul and Barnabas and the apostles and leaders there. This was to discern the mind of God and come to a resolution that could be distributed throughout the church with apostolic authority. From the account Luke gives us of the meeting in Jerusalem (Acts 15) and Paul's writings about the subject in Galatians, we may discern three main arguments that persuaded them of their conclusions.

The argument from the Spirit

To the Galatians Paul pointed out that the presence of the Spirit in their lives had nothing to do with their keeping the law, but exclusively to do with their faith in Christ: 'Did you receive the Spirit by observing the law, or by believing what you heard?' (Galatians 3:2). It is the gift of the Spirit that demonstrates God's acceptance and approval, for 'if anyone does not have the Spirit of Christ, he does not belong to Christ' (Roman 8:9), and the Spirit had evidently been given to uncircumcised Gentiles without any prior conformity to the law. This being so, circumcision was evidently not necessary to gain God's acceptance and blessing.

This is very similar to the line of reasoning presented by Peter when he persuaded the church in Jerusalem to accept the conversion of Cornelius, the first Gentile convert. Circumcised believers had criticized him for welcoming a Gentile convert, but his response, based on the outpouring of the Holy Spirit on Cornelius and his household, was, 'So if God gave them the same gift as he gave us, who believed in the Lord Jesus Christ, who was I to think that I could oppose God?' (Acts 11:17). This was the more subjective and experiential argument.

The argument from Scripture

To convince Jewish believers of his position, Paul needed to defend his views from their Old Testament Scriptures. He did this by arguing that Abraham was justified by faith and not as a result of observing the law (compare Genesis 15:6 with Galatians 3:6–9). Abraham had been declared righteous *before* his circumcision and not *as a result* of his circumcision. His circumcision had in fact been only a sign of the righteousness with which he was already credited on the basis alone of his faith in God. Paul argues from this that Abraham

> is the father of all who believe but have not been circumcised . . . It was not through law that Abraham and his offspring received the promise that he would be heir of the world, but through the righteousness that comes by faith. (Romans 4:11–13)

This was the more objective and theological argument, sustainable by an appeal to the written Scriptures.

The argument from salvation

Paul states categorically to the Galatians, 'If you let yourselves be circumcised, Christ will be of no value to you at all.' He argues this on the grounds that if circumcision is effective in establishing a relationship with God then Christ is redundant and unnecessary to the process. Their embracing the law therefore is to actively alienate themselves from Christ: 'You who are trying to be justified by law have been alienated from Christ; you have fallen away from grace' (Galatians 5:4). If their keeping of the law is necessary to obtain salvation, then Christ is evidently no longer essential to them.

Salvation is either a result of human activity, in which case Christ is redundant and his cross a wasted gesture, or it is a work of God, in which case any contribution from us is both invalid and unnecessary. The measure to which there is a need for human contribution would be the exact measure of the insufficiency of Christ's work on our behalf. Therefore, Paul argues, if people need to be circumcised as a means to salvation then 'the offence of the cross has been abolished' (Galatians 5:11): the cross strikes dead any sense of self-righteousness. So to establish self-righteousness as a means to a relationship with God is to eliminate the cross – the two are mutually exclusive. The offence of the cross is precisely that it requires no contribution from us, and is thus 'a stumbling-block to Jews' (1 Corinthians 1:23) who prided themselves, as Paul once did, on their accomplishments that set them apart from the rest of humankind for unique acceptance by God.

Updating the controversy

Because of the clarity of Paul's statements, the issue of circumcision is a dead one to most believers today, but legalism is not. The principle established by the Council in Jerusalem and clarified in Paul's writings is that nothing of human origin must or can be added to the sufficiency of the person and work of Jesus Christ in order for us to become a full beneficiary.

Equally serious, however, was the problem addressed by Paul

in Galatia of dependency on human activity that did not stop with the means to *becoming* a Christian, but extended to the means of *being* the Christian a person had already become. Paul refers to the 'foolish Galatians' (Galatians 3:1) because they applied the principle of working for God beyond their initial salvation (justification) to the process of Christian living (sanctification). He challenges them, 'Are you so foolish? After beginning with the Spirit, are you now trying to attain your goal by human effort?' (Galatians 3:3). They had begun with the Spirit, many having been born again under Paul's own earlier ministry in Galatia: their new birth was not in doubt either to them or to the apostle. But now as Christian believers they had become dependent on 'human effort' to attain their goal. Reliance on human effort, in whatever form it appears, is as much a threat to a healthy, sanctifying process of growth in the Christian life as it is to the act of becoming a Christian in the first place. Many believers are quick to denounce good works as a means to salvation, while depending on their own innate abilities to do good as Christians! As the source of our justification is the Lord Jesus Christ, so the source of our sanctification is dependence on the indwelling Holy Spirit of Christ, apart from whose presence and activity we can do nothing (see John 15:5).

There is a temptation to draw clear but artificial distinctions between Paul's teaching on justification, sanctification and glorification. There is of course some difference in the meaning of each word, but each is an expression of a common work of God within the Christian. For convenience we tend to say that *justification* relates to a past event in which we are declared righteous before God; *sanctification* relates to a present ongoing process derived from, and dependent on, our past experience of justification; and *glorification* relates to a future event in which each believer is predestined to share the full restoration of God's righteousness once we have arrived in heaven.

These distinctions may have some helpful ingredients, but there is much more overlap between them than these definitions would allow for. Justification has a future dimension to Paul as well as a past, when, for example, he writes, 'For it is not those who hear the law who are righteous in God's sight, but it is those who obey the law who will be declared righteous' (AV 'shall be justified') (Romans 2:13; see also Galatians 5:4–5). Similarly, he also refers to sanctification as a past event as well as a present process when he writes to the Corinthians, having given a catalogue of sins, 'And that is what some of you were. But you were washed, *you were sanctified*, you were justified in the name of the Lord Jesus Christ and by the Spirit of our God' (1 Corinthians 6:11, my emphasis). To the Thessalonians he gives sanctification a future dimension as well as a past and present when he writes, 'May God himself, the God of peace, sanctify you through and through. May your whole spirit, soul and body be kept blameless at the coming of our Lord Jesus Christ' (1 Thessalonians 5:23).

We must be careful, therefore, not to limit Paul's teaching to the Galatians as applying only to those who were seeking initial salvation by observing the law, for in fact the Galatians fully believed in justification by faith rather than by works. Paul affirms to them, 'We . . . know that a man is not justified by observing the law, but by faith in Jesus Christ' (Galatians 2:15–16). He asks them the rhetorical question 'Did you receive the Spirit by observing the law, or by believing what you heard?' (Galatians 3:2), clearly anticipating their agreement that they had received the Spirit on the basis of their believing what they heard and not on observing the law. He then chastises them, for, having received the Spirit by faith, they are now trying to live the Christian life by 'observing the law'.

The bigger problem Paul addresses, therefore, lay not with those who were as yet unsaved, but with those who were already in Christ and who were trying to attain their goal of pleasing God by human effort, human discipline and human activity, rather than on the basis of the working of the indwelling Spirit. It is this temptation that remains a real one today, as it has through history, and one that must be resisted and spurned. Any *addition* to Christ is by definition a *subtraction* from him, for any needed addition can only be a reflection of a sense of his insufficiency.

The problem is that when we attach any addition to faith in Christ as necessary for effective Christian living, the addition often becomes the means whereby our Christianity is defined. Christ plus circumcision is a dead issue to most of us now, but Christ plus a certain mode of baptism is not; Christ plus speaking in tongues is not; Christ plus a right understanding of election is not; Christ plus a particular doctrine of the church is not. The problem is that whatever we add to Christ becomes our defining point. Although we claim to be 'all one in Christ' our fellowship with one another is based on our common agreement about the 'additions' to faith in Christ we see as necessary. So some believers meet as 'Baptists', their very name defining their common ground regarding the essential nature of a certain mode of baptism; some meet as 'Pentecostals' defining their common ground as relating to events on the Day of Pentecost; some meet as 'Congregationalists' or 'Presbyterians' defining their common ground as a view of church government, and so on.

It is not that any of these things are unimportant, for in fact each of the above is very important, which is why they take on such significance for some Christians. Scripture does address those issues and we have to know how to respond rightly to them. My point is that the real problem arises when the issues that make us distinct from one another become our defining point and thus contain the latent inherent danger of taking

priority in our identity. These issues then become more fought
over than those that make us distinct from the world. It is the
same spirit Paul fought in the churches of Antioch, Jerusalem,
Galatia and many other places where the tendency repeatedly
expressed itself. In his day this focused primarily on the issue of
the law and its expression in circumcision, but we must be
equally diligent about the same seductive spirit in our day,
though it may express itself in a whole variety of other ways.

Essentially the issue is this: What are the grounds on which
we may please God? Are there things we do *for God*: *our* discipline, *our* obedience, *our* doctrinal purity, *our* evangelism, *our*
strategies or *our* generosity? Or do the things that please God
derive from what we allow him to do *for us*: *his* strength in place
of our weakness, *his* riches in place of our poverty, and *his*
wisdom in place of our folly? When John penned the letter from
Jesus to the church in Ephesus he was able to commend it for

> your deeds, your hard work and your perseverance. I know that you
> cannot tolerate wicked men, that you have tested those who claim
> to be apostles but are not, and have found them false. You have per-
> severed and have endured hardships for my name, and have not
> grown weary. (Revelation 2:2–3)

We would commend a church with that kind of reputation and
admire it for its disciplined perseverance and doctrinal accu-
racy. There was just one problem, but it was the one problem
that undermined and devalued everything else that was good in
the church in Ephesus. They had forgotten and forsaken Jesus!
'Yet I hold this against you: You have forsaken your first love'
(Revelation 2:4). Every outward appearance may be good,
impressive and commendable, but if the church is not primarily an expression of Jesus himself, whose body the church is; if
it is not fulfilling the desires of the head of that body, which is

Christ himself; if it is not operating in the power of the life of the body, which is the Holy Spirit who inhabits the body, then, says Jesus, 'I will come to you and remove your lampstand from its place' (2:5), meaning in effect, 'I will switch you off!' The need of this doctrinally pure and hard-working church was to 'repent and return', and to get back to a love relationship with Jesus himself that would be expressed in dependency on him alone.

The main thrust of Paul's message is not primarily to do with justification by faith. That is the way in, and needs to be repeatedly made clear. But that is only one expression of a larger underlying theme that permeates his writings – the complete sufficiency of Christ for salvation, and then for life and conduct. 'But if you are led by the Spirit, you are not under law' he told the Galatians (Galatians 5:18). Behaviour that pleases God is 'fruit of the Spirit' (5:22). It is not the fruit of the Christian, for these qualities are impossible, by definition, apart from the enabling Spirit, and represent nothing less than an expression of the character of Christ within us.

There is of course a personal discipline to be exercised by the Christian and Paul encourages that (see 1 Corinthians 9:24–27). But it is a discipline that 'works out' godliness, not one that works it in. Paul writes to the Philippians:

> Therefore, my dear friends, as you have always obeyed – not only in my presence, but now much more in my absence – continue to work out your salvation with fear and trembling, for it is God who works in you to will and to act according to his good purpose. (Philippians 2:12–13)

What we are to 'work out' is a result of what God 'works in' us. When we drive a car, all the power necessary to take the car along the road is under the bonnet. The power is not in the driver but in the engine. The driver will make no contribution by sitting behind the wheel and imitating the noise of the engine! He or she must acknowledge that the power under the bonnet is sufficient to propel the car along the road, but the task then is to bring about the circumstances whereby the power of the engine is translated into the movement of the car. The driver has to put the car into gear, release the clutch and steer it down the road. The engine works under the bonnet and the driver's task is to 'work out' that power into the constructive movement of the car towards its destination. The driver must be alert and disciplined, but it is not the driver who gives the car its capability to perform.

In a similar way the Christian must be alert and disciplined, but human ability does not enable us to live the Christian life. As the engine provides the car's capability to move and perform, so it is Christ living in us who is our capability to live and perform. In the ministry of Paul, anything that threatened, undermined or replaced this central tenet of the Christian faith was to be thoroughly repudiated. His own background of self-induced righteousness and the realization that it was all 'rubbish' so that 'whatever was to my profit I now consider loss for the sake of Christ' (Philippians 3:7), was an added compelling motivation to save others from the same fruitless effort. He did not mean by that statement that he would give up everything *for* Christ, as in some sacrificial act, but that he would give up everything to be replaced *by* Christ, so that 'I no longer live, but Christ lives in me' (Galatians 2:20).

This issue, as in Paul's day, continues to be one of the biggest stumbling blocks to effective Christian living, and needs to be constantly and repeatedly addressed both within the life of the individual and in the corporate life of the church.

10

Union with Christ

The theology of the apostle Paul was not formulated in his study but in his evangelistic exploits on the mission field. He did not sort out his doctrines to make them tidy or even to give them systematic form, much less to stereotype the kindness and grace of God, but he formulated them to address the crying needs of the people to whom he ministered. This is why, unlike the professional theologian's, Paul's doctrines are about life, behaviour, victorious living, and enjoying the presence and activity of God in the real world. He did not set out to write handbooks of Christian doctrine, for his letters were provoked by the need to address particular situations and problems that had arisen in the churches to which he wrote.

We may never have known what Paul believed about the Lord's Supper had some believers in Corinth not acted irresponsibly when they met to celebrate it. If it were not for the Judaizers who insisted on circumcising Gentiles, thus provoking the letter to the Galatians, we would know little about Paul's view of the place of the law in Christian experience. An emerging heresy in Colosse provoked Paul's letter to the church in that city, giving us insight into what he believed about the undermining of the pre-eminence and centrality of Christ. We would not know Paul's stance on the gift of tongues, had not some Christians in Corinth gone overboard in the use of this gift, provoking Paul to rebuke and correct them. As we have seen, the letter to the Romans stands alone of all Paul's letters in not being provoked by a particular pastoral concern for the people to whom he was writing.

We must beware, therefore, of attempting to put Paul's teaching into a watertight system of theology (which he himself did not do). But we must, at the same time, seek to understand the major concerns and thrust of his ministry. Interestingly, no matter what is his starting point, Paul always returns to the central issues of the gospel, and sheer repetition alone would give us a good indication of what was central to his thought. Paul's primary message is the righteousness of God, as we have discussed; a righteousness both imputed to us as an accomplished act on the grounds of faith, and then imparted experientially as an ongoing process, also on the grounds of faith, 'For in the gospel a righteousness from God is revealed, a righteousness that is by faith' (Romans 1:17). At the heart of this experience of God's righteousness, however, is the believer's union with Christ.

For many years following the Reformation of the sixteenth century, Protestant theology concentrated on Paul's doctrine of justification by faith, and understandably so. The rediscovery of this cardinal truth of the New Testament opened the floodgate for the Reformation and represented a liberation from the tyranny of a justification by works to which the church had succumbed for so long. More recent scholarship in the past century, however, has shown that valuable and vital as the theme of justification by faith is in the writings of the apostle Paul, the heart of Paul's teaching about the Christian life is union with Christ.[1] As Professor James Stewart has written:

> If one seeks for the most characteristic sentences the apostle ever wrote, they will be found, not where he is refuting the legalists, or vindicating his apostleship, or meditating on eschatological hopes, or giving practical ethical guidance to the Church, but where his intense intimacy with Christ comes to expression. Everything that religion meant for Paul is focused for us in the great words: 'I live, yet not I, but Christ lives in me.'[2]

To be in union with Christ is for Christ to be in us and for us to be in Christ. It is the fulfilment of Jesus' promise to his disciples 'On that day you will realize that I am in my Father, and you are in me, and I am in you' (John 14:20). The term 'in Christ' (or 'in him' or the combination of 'in' with some designation for Christ) is used some 200 times by Paul and is the most characteristic phrase of his terminology. The term does not originate with Paul, however, for Jesus taught:

> Remain in me [or some translations: 'Abide in me'], and I will remain [abide] in you . . . If a man remains in me and I in him, he will bear much fruit; apart from me you can do nothing. (John 15:4–5)

The source of fruit is the life released by our abiding in Christ and his abiding in us. There are two invitations of Jesus in which the whole of the Christian life may be seen to be encompassed. His first invitation is 'Come to me' (Matthew 11:28),

---

[1] See, for example, James S. Stewart, *A Man in Christ* (Hodder and Stoughton, 1935). I am indebted to this book for its clear argument of the centrality of union with Christ to Paul's thought.

[2] *Ibid.*, p. 147.

and his second 'Remain in me' (John 15:4). If we understand and respond to both of these invitations we are on track to enjoying the full orb of all he has to give to us.

Abiding in Christ

What does it mean to be 'in Christ'? Paul explains this to be the work of the Holy Spirit; in fact the result of baptism by the Spirit. 'For we were all baptised by one Spirit into one body [Christ] – whether Jews or Greeks, slave or free – and we were all given the one Spirit to drink' (1 Corinthians 12:13). The infusion of the Holy Spirit into a person necessarily unites them in union with Christ, for through this very act, his life now indwells them.

Let me attempt to illustrate this point. I have a friend who suffered an accident while working on a piece of heavy machinery and three of the four fingers on his left hand were completely cut off. He picked up the severed fingers in his right hand and went for help! He was taken to hospital, where through delicate microsurgery his fingers were sewn back on to his hand. In the course of time he regained sufficient feeling and movement so that today he has almost complete use of them again. When his fingers had been cut off and before the microsurgery had taken place his fingers were to all appearances dead. They lay lifeless on the floor. If you stroked them they would not respond, if you used one of them to stir a cup of tea it would not protest or react in pain from the boiling heat, if you used them as doorstoppers they would not complain, for they were dead, detached from their only source of life, the body. This is similar to the natural condition of human beings separated from God. Paul, speaking of the natural condition of every human being, said, 'In Adam all die' (1 Corinthians 15:22). He writes to the Romans, 'The wages of sin is death' (Romans 6:23) – a present-tense statement, not referring to the future consequences of sin, but to the present condition in which every human is to be found by nature. This death is not physical but spiritual, for it is to be 'separated from the life of God' (Ephesians 4:18).

There is only one remedy for death – and that is life! The need of every human being is to be reconciled to God in order to become a recipient of his life, the life from which we were originally separated. The successful act of stitching my friend's fingers back on to his hand meant that two things took place simultaneously: the fingers became infused again with the life of the body, they became alive, and the body received its fingers back to be part again of its overall capability.

In a similar way, when we, through repentance and faith, are reconciled to God two things take place. First, we receive the actual life of God, who comes by his Holy Spirit to inhabit our humanity and live the life of Jesus in us, which is what it means to be 'born again'. Secondly, Jesus Christ receives us as part of his body, for we are brought into union with him. By definition, what constitutes my body is that which my life inhabits. If I had an artificial leg or a glass eye it would be useful to me but would not be part of my body. I could detach the leg at night or replace it when it wore out or a better model came along. It would not be my body because my life would not be in it.

In a similar way, what makes the church the body of Christ is that it is inhabited by the Spirit of Christ and each member of his body shares together his life. It is this union with Christ that makes a person a Christian, for Paul writes, 'And if anyone does not have the Spirit of Christ, he does not belong to Christ' (Romans 8:9). Christ being in us and we being in Christ are two separate sides of one coin, for although they are distinct they must of necessity be simultaneous in experience. My friend could not have life put into his fingers without his fingers being reattached to his hand, for the simple reason that the life of his fingers is the life of his body. Similarly, we cannot be indwelt by the Spirit of God without being brought into union with Christ, for what unites us to him and makes us one with him is the presence of his life within us, which also makes us one with all those who are similarly indwelt by his Spirit. We have become participants in his one body.

Christ being in us is the result of receiving the Spirit (Acts 2:38; Romans 8:9). Our being in Christ is the result of baptism by the Spirit (1 Corinthians 12:13). The first gives us *power*, the second gives us *purpose*. The Spirit's indwelling gives us power in much the same way as the life of my friend inhabiting his fingers gives them power, strength and ability. Our being in Christ gives us purpose, in a similar way that once the fingers of my friend were reattached to his hand, they were able to function in harmony with the rest of the body to fulfil the purposes of the head. Paul describes this as 'clothing yourselves with Christ' and it is the basis of the oneness with each other that is the characteristic of all true Christians, 'for all of you who were baptised into Christ have clothed yourselves with Christ. There is neither Jew nor Greek, slave nor free, male nor female, for you are all one in Christ Jesus' (Galatians 3:27–28).

Identification with Christ

Union with Christ in the writings of Paul not only involves the fact that believers share together the indwelling life of Christ as the essential dynamic of the Christian life, but is also an identification with the work of Christ applied retrospectively, in particular to our union with Christ in his death and resurrection. Paul writes to the Romans:

> Or don't you know that all of us who were baptised into Christ Jesus were baptised into his death? We were therefore buried with

him through baptism into death in order that, just as Christ was raised from the dead through the glory of the Father, we too may live a new life.

If we have been united with him like this in his death, we will certainly also be united with him in his resurrection. For we know that our old self was crucified with him so that the body of sin might be done away with, that we should no longer be slaves to sin – because anyone who has died has been freed from sin.

Now if we died with Christ, we believe that we will also live with him. (Romans 6:3–8)

This reference to baptism is not about water baptism, though baptism in water is the proper outward physical expression of inner spiritual baptism to which he refers here. There is 'one baptism' (Ephesians 4:5) says Paul, yet he speaks of both water baptism and Spirit baptism indicating that one (water baptism) is an expression of the other (Spirit baptism) and the two should not be separated. By one Spirit we are baptized into Christ, Paul tells the Corinthians, and now asks the Romans whether they realize that this baptism by the Spirit into Christ is also a baptism into his death, and that by being baptized into his death we have 'died to sin'.

There have been different understandings of this passage, some popular interpretations seeing this as a subjective, experiential death to sin, related to the sanctification of the believer, whereby through a particular experience of God's grace the Christian may be liberated from the power of sin in his or her life. This is of course a very attractive notion, but does not seem to stand up to a close scrutiny of what Paul is actually saying. The 'death to sin' that is to be experienced and enjoyed by the Christian is identical to the death to sin experienced by Christ, for having said of Christ, 'The death he died, he died to sin once for all' (Romans 6:10), Paul then says of us, 'In the same way, count yourselves dead to sin' (Romans 6:11). Our death to sin is 'in the same way' as Christ's death to sin. Therefore, to understand what it is for us to 'die to sin' we must understand what it was for Christ to 'die to sin'.

Christ did not die to the power of sin in his life (as is the application often made to the Christian) for he was as free as any man could be from its power for the whole of his life, but his death was related to the consequences of sin. What are the consequences of sin? Later in the same chapter Paul answers our question: 'For the wages of sin is death' (6:23). This is the unavoidable consequence of sin, a state into which we are born and destined to remain if left to ourselves. When Christ died he took on himself the just wrath of God against sin so that 'God made him who had no sin to be sin for us' (2 Corinthians 5:21), and took the full, undiluted penalty for sin.

To be 'baptised into his death', and to be 'united with him in his death' means that our identification with Christ is such that what was true of Christ now becomes credited as true of us. When Paul writes, 'I have been crucified with Christ and I no longer live' (Galatians 2:20), he is not referring to a personal event in his life whereby on a certain date in his experience he was 'crucified', but is referring to the event outside the city walls of Jerusalem that took place before Paul ever knew Christ for himself. When he came to be 'in Christ', all that was true of Christ became retrospectively true of him.

I have often been asked, 'How do I die to sin?' or 'How do I crucify myself?' Think hard about the question as a literal proposition! How could someone crucify themselves? It is impossible. We might put a nail through one hand, but what would we do about the other? Free the first hand so that we can nail the second? Then what would we do about the first? Free the second to nail the first? It is physically impossible to crucify ourselves. We have to *be* crucified. And the great news is that we have been! When was I crucified? Two thousand years ago, on a Roman cross outside the city walls of Jerusalem in the person of the Lord Jesus Christ.

When Paul encourages us to 'count yourselves dead to sin', he is not speaking about an act of sanctification that is subsequent to our salvation, but the act of justification that is the very substance of our salvation whereby in God's reckoning we are legally recognized to have 'been crucified with Christ and I no longer live'.

His cross is our death

We may ask a Christian, 'What is going to happen to you on account of your sin?' He or she may legitimately answer: 'I have to suffer God's sentence on my sin and die, but in point of fact, I have already done so. Two thousand years ago I was nailed to a cross and died as a result of my sin, so I no longer live as far as my guilt is concerned – I have died for that and its penalty is paid in full. The power of sin has taken its course and I have died. And yet I am still alive, and it is now impossible for me to die again for sin, because in addition to being united with Christ in his death, I am also united to Christ in his resurrection. His death became my death, and his life has become my life, and that life is untouchable by sin, "For we know that since Christ was raised from the dead, he cannot die again; death no longer has mastery over him" (Romans 6:9), and I am completely free!'

Our freedom from sin does not refer to our behaviour, but to our status before God. All that is true of Christ is now true of us, and my destiny is inextricably linked to his. This is why Paul can write, 'Therefore, there is now no condemnation for those who are in Christ Jesus' (Romans 8:1), not because we do not sin, for in this life Paul is unambiguous about our continual conflict with sin, but because Christ has died for sin and paid its debt in full as our substitute and risen victoriously from the dead, never to die again. As Christ is not condemned and what is true of him is true of us, we too have died and risen with him and are not condemned. The apostle John goes so far as to speak of having confidence on the Day of Judgement on account of our union with Christ when he writes, 'In this way, love is made complete among us so that we will have confidence on the day of judgment, because in this world we are like him' (1 John 4:17). Our union with Christ is such that in God's reckoning of us, 'we are like him'.

His resurrection is our life

But there is more than our standing before God at stake. Paul's message includes the fact that out of our union with Christ, all the resources necessary for life and godliness are made available to us: 'you are in Christ Jesus, who has become for us wisdom from God – that is, our righteousness, holiness and redemption' (1 Corinthians 1:30). Furthermore, all the promises of God will find their fulfilment, 'For no matter how many promises God has made, they are "Yes" in Christ' (2 Corinthians 1:20). No wonder he writes, 'Therefore, if anyone is in Christ, he is a new creation; the old has gone, the new has come!' (2 Corinthians 5:17).

In the opening section of his letter to the Ephesians Paul speaks most fully of all the blessing available to us by our union with Christ, beginning with the comprehensive statement 'Praise be to the God and Father of our Lord Jesus Christ, who has blessed us in the heavenly realms *with every spiritual blessing in Christ*' (Ephesians 1:3, my emphasis), and in the verses that follow he elaborates some of these *spiritual blessings* that are ours in Christ.

Linking what Paul has said with the teaching of Jesus, it is only as we understand our union with Christ and live in the good of all the resources that we have in him, that we can live effectively, victoriously and fruitfully:

> Remain in me, and I will remain in you. No branch can bear fruit by itself; it must remain in the vine. Neither can you bear fruit unless you remain in me.
>
> I am the vine; you are the branches. If a man remains in me and I in him, he will bear much fruit; apart from me you can do nothing. (John 15:4–5)

We will never understand Paul unless we realize that union with Christ is both the key to everything else in his life and to unlocking the full orb of his message.

11

Civil War in the Soul

Paul held little hope of any intrinsic improvement of the human heart. He laments in his letter to the Romans, 'I know that nothing good lives in me, that is, in my sinful nature. For I have the desire to do what is good, but I cannot carry it out' (Romans 7:18). This is not a statement of what Paul *used to be* before he came to know Christ, but of what he *continued to be* in his natural self, after he had come to Christ and of what he would *continue to be* for the rest of his life. The term 'sinful nature' used in the NIV is a translation of just one word in the original Greek, the word 'flesh'. 'Sinful nature' is an Augustinian term coined in the fifth century, and has served as a useful description. The word 'flesh', however, when it occurs in this context, refers not to the physical body, but to all that a person is in themselves apart from the presence of God within them. To live 'in the flesh' is to live in the spirit of independence and self-reliance founded on self-accomplishments, rather than in a spirit of dependence on and obedience to God. It refers to the bankruptcy of human resources, human ability, human skill and human capability, when detached from the enabling grace, presence and power of God.

It is this sense of despair over any hope of the natural person being able to function as God intends on the basis of human resources that lies behind Paul's view of humanity. This may at first seem a rather pessimistic view, but it is entirely realistic and accurate. Apart from the clear revelation of this in Scripture, and God's provision of his Holy Spirit, we would have neither the grounds nor the courage to face this truth about the human condition. Jeremiah wrote long before Paul's day:

> The heart is deceitful above all things
>   and beyond cure.
> Who can understand it? (Jeremiah 17:9)

Most disillusionment with the Christian life has its origin in an expectancy that, given a bit of time, discipline and the grace of God, our hearts will somehow improve and our natural selves will grow in godliness. But the Christian life, according to Paul, does not involve the *eradication* or the *suppression* of sin, but its *counteraction*, by the indwelling presence of the Spirit. The reality of our sinful nature remains within us throughout this life, but is counteracted by the indwelling Holy Spirit.

Paul speaks of this particularly in his letters to the Galatians and Romans. To the Galatians he writes:

For the sinful nature desires what is contrary to the Spirit, and the Spirit what is contrary to the sinful nature. They are in conflict with each other, so that you do not do what you want. (Galatians 5:17)

This statement is true for every Christian, no matter how long he or she has been a believer. When the Holy Spirit comes to indwell the Christian at the point of new birth, there begins a civil war in the soul that will continue right through the course of life. The natural flesh is in conflict with the Spirit and the Spirit with the natural flesh, and there is a relentless, never-ending battle 'so that you do not do what you want'.

Paul gives a graphic description of this battle in his own life in Romans 7:15–23. He acknowledges that there are things we know are wrong and resolve never to do, but despite the best intentions, we do them. There are things we know are right and determine and promise ourselves we will do them, but we don't! This is an experience every one of us shares in common. Paul's explanation for this is interesting. Twice he states, 'It is no longer I myself who do it, but it is sin living in me' (Romans 7:17). This sounds rather like an irresponsible excuse and therefore a cop-out! If someone were to punch me on the nose and then explain, 'It is not I doing this but sin living in me that is doing it,' I would find this difficult to accept as a legitimate explanation. Especially if they then do it again . . . and again. What does Paul mean?

The law of sin

He is not speaking of sin as *actions* at this point but as a *principle*, which he describes as the *law of sin* (Romans 7:23). This is a natural law that operates in the heart of every person. It may best be illustrated as being like the law of gravity that determines a constant downward pull. All of us are subject to this law of sin, as a consequence of the fallen nature with which we are born. We will never truly understand ourselves until we know and accept this fact about ourselves, as Paul summarizes: 'I know that nothing good lives in me, that is, in my sinful nature' (Romans 7:18). If we fail to believe this, we will attempt to refine ourselves, we will make repeated promises to God about how good we are going to be from this moment on, we will go through a process of dedicating ourselves to God one month and rededicating ourselves the next, then rededicating our rededication, but despite the greatest intentions, we will fail! We should not be too disappointed by that, however, for we will never be a bigger failure than the one God already knows us to be. God offers no hope to the natural person for any progress in righteousness on the basis of human strength, human resources or determined dedication to become what he wants us to be.

We may in the course of time become disillusioned with ourselves, but God will never be disillusioned about us for the simple reason that he doesn't suffer from any illusions about us in the first place! It is we who think that perhaps, with a little more effort on our part, a little more discipline, a little more determination, a little more dedication and resolve, we may finally be able to accomplish something that forwards our sanctification and holiness of life.

But unfortunately, the human heart is corrupt. James asks the question 'What causes fights and quarrels among you?', and then answers it: 'Don't they come from your desires that battle within you?' (James 4:1). Earlier James had written, 'Each one is tempted when, by his own evil desire, he is dragged away and enticed' (James 1:14). It is our own *evil desire* that leads us astray and gets us into trouble. That is why we must be careful not to blame the devil for our sins. Of course the devil attacks and seeks to divert us, but temptation primarily comes from within. If the devil were to die today, we would still sin tomorrow! Much as we may hate sin, the reality is that every temptation we face is, by definition, attractive to us – otherwise it would not be a temptation. The devil is of course active in tempting us, as he was in the experience of Eve before she fell, and supremely in the experience of Jesus who was 'tempted in every way, just as we are . . .' (Hebrews 4:15). His tactic is more to question God, either explicitly, such as to Eve, 'Did God really say . . . ?' (Genesis 3:1) or implicitly, as to Jesus when he queried, '*If* you are the son of God . . .' (Matthew 4:3–6), but the desire for sin which makes temptation so attractive to us comes from our own nature.

Paul is unambiguous about this universal corruption of human nature. If that seems a rather pessimistic and discouraging piece of news, however, we need to recognize that there is an equal and opposing truth, and it is this: the Holy Spirit, who comes to live within each believer in response to their repentance towards God and faith in Jesus Christ, is the complete opposite of everything that we are by nature!

Paul's definition of a Christian is not someone who has had their sins forgiven, but someone who has become indwelt by the Spirit of Jesus Christ. The forgiveness of sin is a necessary means to that end, but in itself does not constitute the new birth. New birth is (by definition) about coming alive. More than experiencing the forgiveness for past sin, it involves regeneration, the receiving of new life, and that new life is the life of Christ, 'And if anyone does not have the Spirit of Christ, he does not belong to Christ' (Romans 8:9). When asking the Corinthians to examine whether they are actually in the faith or not, Paul writes, 'Examine yourselves to see whether you are in the faith; test yourselves. Do you not realize that Christ Jesus is in you – unless, of course, you fail the test?' (2 Corinthians 13:5). To be a Christian is to receive the actual life of God, and for the Holy Spirit to make our bodies his home. The apostle Peter expresses it forcefully when he writes:

> His divine power has given us everything we need for life and godliness through our knowledge of him who called us by his own glory and goodness. Through these he has given us his very great and precious promises, so that through them you may *participate in the divine nature and escape the corruption in the world caused by evil desires*. (2 Peter 1:3–4, my emphasis)

It is through actual participation in the divine nature, the nature of God implanted within us, that we may escape the corruption caused by our evil desires.

It is because his pure, sinless life inhabits our fallen humanity that the conflict between the *flesh* and the *spirit* takes place. It is not that we have two natures and experience a kind of spiritual schizophrenia! We have only one nature, and it is corrupt, but we are indwelt by the Holy Spirit who is the opposite of all that we are by nature. It is of course necessary that we discipline the old nature, but we will not change it.

The law of the Spirit of life

When Paul speaks of the recurring battle with which he struggles, he comes to the conclusion 'What a wretched man I am! Who will rescue me from this body of death?' (Romans 7:24). His question is an important one. He does not cry, '*What* will rescue me?', that is, 'Is there a method, a technique, a programme or an experience that will rescue me from this law of sin?' There are all kinds of remedies made available from time to time in the Christian market place, but they need updating every few years for they do not last and ultimately do not work. Paul's question is far more profound: '*Who* will rescue me?' This requires something much bigger than a technique or programme, or a few do-it-yourself steps; it has to be *someone*! He then immediately answers his own question, 'Thanks be to God – through Jesus Christ our Lord!' (Romans 7:25). Only Jesus Christ can liberate us from ourselves, and he does so by counteracting the law of sin with a higher law, for he goes on to say, 'Through Christ Jesus the law of the Spirit of life set me free from the law of sin and death' (Romans 8:2).

I am actually writing the first draft of this chapter over the Atlantic Ocean sitting in a Boeing 777 on a flight from Chicago to London. Needing to return to my home after preaching at a conference in the United States, I knew when I got up this morning that there was no possibility of my jumping the

Atlantic Ocean, for the simple reason that there is a natural law, gravity, that will prevent me from doing so. If I make any attempt to go up, it will make sure that I come down! But I happen to know too that there is a more powerful law than the law of gravity, called the law of aerodynamics. This is the law that enables an aeroplane to counteract the law of gravity and fly.

So I went to O'Hare airport in Chicago, boarded a Boeing 777, sat down and fastened my seat belt. The aircraft moved away from the gate, went to the end of the runway, sped along the tarmac and, leaving the ground, soared into the air. Right now, at a height of 33,000 feet I am able to say, 'The law of aerodynamics has set me free from the law of gravity.' Paul writes, 'The law of the Spirit of life in Christ Jesus set me free from the law of sin and death' (Romans 8:2). The aircraft has not eradicated, suspended or suppressed gravity; it has counteracted it. The gospel does not include an eradication of the old nature in this life (that is held in prospect for heaven), but it does include a counteraction of the law of sin by the inner pull of the law of the Spirit of life in Christ. Paul writes to the Philippians, 'It is God who works in you to will and to act according to his good purpose' (Philippians 2:13). Both the desire and the ability to live according to God's good purpose is a work of God himself within us and we are utterly and completely dependent on him for that.

Going back to the analogy of the law of aerodynamics setting me free from gravity, although it is true as I write this page that I am 33,000 feet above the Atlantic, not for one moment of this journey am I able to fly. I am being flown. There is a difference. I did not go to the check-in desk in Chicago and say, 'Could you please give me the ability to fly to London?' They would probably look at me rather strangely and say, 'I am sorry, but we cannot give you the ability to fly anywhere, but we can fly you.'

God does not *give* us strength, he *is* our strength. Many times in the Old Testament in particular, writers state, 'The Lord is my strength' (see, for example, Exodus 15:2; Psalms 28:7; 118:14; Isaiah12:2; Habakkuk 3:19). He does not so much impart strength to us as make his own presence within us to be our strength, as our dependency is placed exclusively on him.

So what do we do about the old nature? Paul is clear about this – our old nature is crucified with Christ. He writes, 'Those who belong to Christ Jesus have crucified the sinful nature with its passions and desires' (Galatians 5:24). Earlier in the same letter Paul says, 'I have been crucified with Christ and I no longer live, but Christ lives in me' (Galatians 2:20); and in Romans he exhorts us to 'count yourselves dead to sin' (Romans 6:11). What does this mean? It is important to observe that whenever Paul speaks of our crucifixion it is always in the past tense: 'I have been crucified'. As we saw in the last chapter, it is not something we are instructed to do, but something already done. We were crucified two thousand years ago, outside the city walls of Jerusalem where our old natural self received everything it deserved in the person of a substitute, the Lord Jesus Christ. Legally and judicially, everything we deserve as guilty sinners has been meted out to us already. It is not only true that Christ died *for* us, but also that we died *in* him.

Elsewhere in his writings, however, Paul tells us clearly that we are responsible to put to death the misdeeds of the body: 'For if you live according to the sinful nature, you will die; but if by the Spirit you put to death the misdeeds of the body, you will live' (Romans 8:13); and, 'Put to death, therefore, whatever belongs to your earthly nature: sexual immorality, impurity, lust, evil desires and greed, which is idolatry' (Colossians 3:5). That means we must not allow these desires to function, but must knock them on the head and 'put them to death', as an ongoing responsibility.

Our crucifixion with Christ, however, represents our legal status before God. We are judiciously regarded as having paid in full the just penalty for sin, in the person of the Lord Jesus Christ who died as our substitute and representative before God. In Christ, legally, I died. Therefore, although I have to live every day with the reality of my tendency to sin, I am already liberated from the consequences of my sin. This does not mean, as Paul explains in Romans, that this then gives me liberty to sin on the grounds that Christ's death for sin frees me to indulge in it. He responds to that suggestion, 'We died to sin; how can we live in it any longer?' (Romans 6:2). This is not to state the impossibility of living in sin, but the incongruity of it. It has been dealt with in the crucifixion of Christ, which is my crucifixion before God, and therefore the consequences of sin have been fully met and its power broken. Later he adds to show that although 'crucified', the battle with sin in personal experience continues, 'Therefore do not let sin reign in your mortal body so that you obey its evil desires' (Romans 6:12). We battle with the 'evil desires' of human nature on the one hand, and the obligation to 'not let sin reign' on the other.

Although it is the presence of the Holy Spirit within the Christian that counteracts the sinful nature, this does not imply that we have nothing to do but to sit back in passive dependency on God. We are to operate in an active sense of obedience and trust where our dependency on the Holy Spirit is in the context of necessary obedience to his instructions.

Renewing the mind

In Romans 8, the great chapter on the Holy Spirit in Paul's systematic presentation of the gospel, he talks about the crucial role of the mind in relation to living in the Spirit:

> Those who live according to the sinful nature have their *minds* set
> on what that nature desires; but those who live in accordance with
> the Spirit have their *minds* set on what the Spirit desires. (Romans
> 8:5, my emphasis)

The word 'repent' literally means 'to change the mind'. In the
original Greek version of the New Testament the word *meta-noia* is a combination of two words, *meta* (to change), and *noia*
(the mind). Repentance is not essentially something we feel or
do; it is something we think. It is a change of mind that leads
inevitably to a change of behaviour, but the change of behavi-our is only a symptom of the change of mind. That is why John
the Baptist told his listeners, 'Produce fruit in keeping with
repentance' (Luke 3:8). The change in behaviour he demanded
of them was not the substance of their repentance, but the fruit
of their change of mind about themselves, about their sin and
about God.

If a person becomes a Christian by an *act of repentance*, the
mind is taken up with things of the Spirit by an *attitude of
repentance*, helping that person to live the Christian life. Paul
later exhorted the Romans to 'be transformed by the renewing
of your mind' (Romans 12:2). We would prefer to be 'trans-formed by a sizzle down the spine' that is cheap, quick and
exciting, but Paul does not offer a 'quick fix' process. Instead,
on the basis of the indwelling presence of the Spirit in our
hearts, there is to be an ongoing process of growth as our minds
are moulded by truth. That is why there can be no substitute in
spiritual growth for spending time in the word of God.

The Spirit and the word

There are several striking similarities between passages Paul
writes to the Ephesians and the Colossians, one of which is

particularly interesting in this context. To the Ephesians he writes:

> Do not get drunk on wine, which leads to debauchery. Instead, *be filled with the Spirit*. Speak to one another with psalms, hymns and spiritual songs. Sing and make music in your heart to the Lord, always giving thanks to God the Father for everything, in the name of our Lord Jesus Christ. (Ephesians 5:18–20, my emphasis)

He then goes on in the following verses to talk about the submission of wives to husbands, children to fathers and slaves to masters as an expression of the fullness of the Spirit.

To the Colossians Paul writes:

> *Let the word of Christ dwell in you richly* as you teach and admonish one another with all wisdom, and as you sing psalms, hymns and spiritual songs with gratitude in your hearts to God. And whatever you do, whether in word or deed, do it all in the name of the Lord Jesus, giving thanks to God the Father through him. (Colossians 3:16–17, my emphasis)

He then also goes on to write, just as he did to the Ephesians, about the mutual submission of wives to husbands, children to fathers and slaves to masters. The context of both statements is similar, but the central imperatives are different. To the Ephesians he says, 'Be filled with the Spirit,' and to the Colossians he says, 'Let the word of Christ dwell in you richly,' with the same consequences for both: speaking, singing and submitting to one another. These verses do not present an either/or means to the lifestyle he advocates, but a mutual relationship of both to each other. We cannot enjoy a sustained filling of the Spirit without letting the word of Christ dwell in us richly, nor will the word of Christ dwell in us richly if we are not filled with the Spirit – each contributes to the other. The word brings us to dependency on the Spirit and the Spirit illuminates and makes living the word. That is why living in the Spirit is directly related by Paul to 'having [our] minds set on what the Spirit desires'.

Paul tells the Romans, 'So then faith cometh by hearing, and hearing by the word of God' (Romans 10:17 AV). As we get to know the word of God, our confidence in God grows and our dependency on him increases. We cannot know more of God than we know of his word! It is in his word that God is revealed to us, and it is there Paul tells us to be a 'workman . . . who correctly handles the word of truth' (2 Timothy 2:15).

Reaping what we sow

While Paul speaks to the Romans about the mind being taken up with either the things of the flesh or the things of the Spirit, to the Galatians he writes about sowing seeds that will germinate and grow into either a destructive, or a life-giving force: 'The one who sows to please his sinful nature, from that nature will reap destruction; the one who sows to please the Spirit, from the Spirit will reap eternal life' (Galatians 6:8). We may sow seeds designed to satisfy and please the flesh, and we will reap the consequences – destruction. Or we may sow seeds designed to satisfy and please the Spirit, and we will reap the consequences – a greater enjoyment of that new quality of life that is the life of God in us, eternal life.

When we find ourselves falling into major areas of sin, it is rarely if ever because the sin has crept up on us and caught us unawares. Long before the events take place we have foolishly sown the seeds that have, in their own time, germinated and produced their fruit. When a Christian of standing falls in some public way, as many sadly have, we may be shocked by it, but we may be fairly sure it did not take place overnight. Long before the events took place, unchecked seeds sown in the soil of their minds germinated in the course of time, came to life and produced their inevitable fruit. Burying sin does not deal with it. Seeds love to be buried – that is when they come alive, grow and reproduce themselves! The only way sin ever leaves our body is through the mouth: 'If we confess our sins, he is faithful and just and will forgive us our sins and purify us from all unrighteousness' (1 John 1:9).

When Paul speaks in Galatians of destruction as the consequence of sowing to the flesh, he is not speaking of eternal damnation, for he is addressing those already indwelt by the Spirit and sealed by his presence as God's people for ever. Rather, it is the same destruction he writes about to the Corinthians when, using a different metaphor, he speaks about the need to construct a building on the foundation of Jesus Christ in their lives:

> If any man builds on this foundation using gold, silver, costly stones, wood, hay or straw, his work will be shown for what it is, because the Day will bring it to light. It will be revealed with fire, and the fire will test the quality of each man's work. If what he has built survives, he will receive his reward. If it is burned up, he will suffer loss; he himself will be saved, but only as one escaping through the flames. (1 Corinthians 3:12–15)

This is a destruction that involves 'escaping through the flames', but with empty hands. To sow seeds that are purely human oriented and detached from God is to sow things that may well 'please the sinful nature' in the short term, but will carry no eternal dimension or quality; on the contrary they will actively rob us of the eternal benefits otherwise in store on the Day of Judgement.

To sow to the Spirit is actively to plant the things of the Spirit. Deliberately to be taken up with those things that please

God and satisfy his agenda is to sow seeds that also germinate, grow and produce the fruit of life in all its fullness, in both the present and future. To love Jesus Christ, to love his word, to live in submission to him, to obey his instructions is to be sowing good seed into good soil. Paul describes the harvest of this good seed to the Galatians, 'But the fruit of the Spirit is love, joy, peace, patience, kindness, goodness, faithfulness, gentleness and self-control. Against such things there is no law' (Galatians 5:22–23). There he lists nine qualities, but he does not say, 'The fruits of the Spirit *are* . . .' in the plural. Instead, he says, 'The fruit of the Spirit *is* . . .' in the singular. We may reduce these qualities to just one word and call the fruit of the Spirit 'character'. We may be even more specific than that and say, 'The fruit of the Spirit is the character of Jesus Christ.' God holds no greater ambition for any of his people than for them to become like his Son as a result of the presence and working of his Spirit in them. These qualities are the fruit of the Spirit, therefore they are divine in origin and supernatural in expression.

The harvest, however, does not come overnight. Paul says in this context to the Galatians, 'Let us not become weary in doing good, for at the proper time we will reap a harvest if we do not give up' (Galatians 6:9). God is totally committed to our godliness, to reproducing the character of his Son in us – and he is doing it. We will be the last people to see this in ourselves for we will be conscious of the old nature fighting against the Spirit to keep us from doing what we would like to do, and we will be able to present every reason in the world to be discouraged. But others will see Christ in us. We will be conscious of the battle; they will see the victory. We will know the struggle; they will see the rest. That is why our task is to 'fix our eyes on Jesus' (Hebrews 12:2), be taken up with him and his interests, and leave the consequences with God.

In a beautiful sentence in the best-known of all psalms, David writes: 'You prepare a table before me in the presence of my enemies' (Psalm 23:5). In that sentence there is both a feast and a fight. We may enjoy the table spread before us, the feast, but it is in the presence of the enemies, the fight. The fight is persistent, but so is the feast. His victory is enjoyed in the midst of our conflict, his strength in the context of our weakness, and his riches in place of our poverty.

Paul is unambiguous about this. The civil war in the soul will be an ongoing reality until the day we die, but so will be the liberating presence and counteraction of the Holy Spirit who alone is equal to the task.

12

The Strength of Weakness

In our twenty-first century, weakness is not a virtue. We find therefore a major conflict with our normal pattern of thinking and expectancy when we discover Paul saying, 'I delight in weaknesses' (2 Corinthians 12:10); 'We are glad whenever we are weak' (13:9); and, 'If I must boast, I will boast of the things that show my weakness' (11:30). Far from being a source of embarrassment to him or a disqualification for his ministry, Paul's weakness is his badge of office and paradoxically, the very grounds of his confidence. To the apostle Paul, human weakness is the platform on which the power of God is exhibited in the world, the safest channel for the demonstration of divine power, for 'when I am weak, then am I strong' (12:10).

Paul is his most eloquent on the power of weakness when writing his epistles to the Corinthians, where he speaks positively of weakness on 29 occasions. Some in Corinth were calling Paul's apostleship into question on account of his weak appearance (see 2 Corinthians 10:10; 1 Corinthians 2:1–5) and his frequent suffering, which discredited him in the eyes of his antagonists, who supposed the idea of a 'suffering apostle' to be a contradiction in terms. Earlier too the Jews had rejected the idea of a 'suffering Messiah' as an absurdity, and some more recently reject the idea of a suffering Christian! Paul's response, in complete contrast to this false notion, was to regard his sufferings not as discrediting his apostleship, but commending it when he writes, 'If I must boast, I will boast of the things that show my weakness' (2 Corinthians 11:30; see also 2 Corinthians 4:7–17; 6:3–10). He presents us with a catalogue of events that would cause many of us to doubt the presence of God, or at the very least the care of God, in our lives. If Paul was on a divine mission, if his God had promised to supply all his needs (Philippians 4:19), if he could instruct others, 'Do not be anxious about anything' (Philippians 4:6), why was he given the 39 lashes on 5 occasions, why was he beaten with rods, flogged with whips, stoned until he was left for dead in a pool of his own blood? Why did he have days with no food on his table, and another time with no clothes on his back, and why did his boats so frequently sink (2 Corinthians 11:23–29)? Furthermore, as God had used him in the healing of sicknesses in others, why did he himself not radiate abundant health instead of being so ill in Galatia that his presence was a trial to those with whom he stayed (see Galatians 4:14)? Not only did some of Paul's contemporaries have difficulty reconciling all of this with marks of authentic Christianity and a genuine ministry, but also the assumption that health, wealth and prosperity are evidence of God's blessing has characterized some Christians down through the years, and especially in today's more affluent and comfortable world.

The remarkable thing is that Paul extols his suffering as a mark of the genuineness of his apostleship. It is not just that he can explain it away, or give anecdotes to prove these bad things all worked to a good end eventually. Many of them stand alone as bad experiences and cannot be justified by any sense of good that subsequently came out of them.

A thorn in the flesh

Paul himself was tempted to regard such hindrances and difficulties as handicaps to his ministry, until God taught his servant an important lesson when he refused to relieve him of a 'thorn in the flesh'. Paul explains to the Corinthians:

> To keep me from becoming conceited because of these surpassingly great revelations, there was given me a thorn in my flesh, a messenger of Satan, to torment me. Three times I pleaded with the Lord to take it away from me. But he said to me, 'My grace is sufficient for you, for my power is made perfect in weakness.' Therefore I will boast all the more gladly about my weaknesses, so that Christ's power may rest on me. (2 Corinthians 12:7–9)

He doesn't tell us what this 'thorn' was, but as it was 'in my flesh' it was almost certainly something physical. There has been huge speculation as to the nature of the thorn, and as someone else has suggested, if we were to list all the possible physical ailments that have been proposed it would read like a medical dictionary! One popular and plausible idea is that he had a speech impediment, which is why his first appearances among new people were not impressive, giving rise to the statement 'In person he is unimpressive and his speaking amounts to nothing' (2 Corinthians 10:10). His own assessment to the Corinthians was, 'When I came to you, brothers, I did not come with eloquence or superior wisdom as I proclaimed to you the testimony about God' (1 Corinthians 2:1). This explanation may account for his apparent denial of eloquence in person in contrast with his obvious eloquence in writing.

Some have suggested that Paul's thorn in the flesh was not a physical problem at all but was his sinful nature, which Paul frequently described by the same word 'flesh',[1] and that the struggle which had its source in Satan was to do with temptation and sin. There are two problems associated with this interpretation. First, if this is so, Paul is asking for a removal of the pull of his old nature – which he never tells his readers to expect. Secondly, the response God gave to Paul would mean that in the apostle's sinful indulgence God's strength is made perfect. As Paul neither offers nor expects any means of escape from the battle with the sinful nature (see Galatians 5:17), it would indicate that his use of the word 'flesh' in this context must be something more than just the common experience of battling with temptation. But the idea cannot be absolutely ruled out.

Others have proposed that Paul is referring to his persecutions from which he sought deliverance, or that it was his single status that tormented him. It has even been suggested that this was evidence he was married, but that his wife had left him after he had become a Christian in Damascus and he wanted her back![2] All of these are only guesses, however, as Paul himself does not tell us the nature of the 'thorn'. What he does tell us is that it had a weakening effect on him, and in his own judgement he would be much the better person if the problem were resolved or completely removed from him.

It therefore seems most likely that his reference to the flesh is of some physical disability with which he struggled. There is a strong possibility that Paul suffered from severe eye trouble that hindered him in his ministry. When he spoke of his illness being a trial when he was in Galatia, he said, 'I can testify that,

---

[1] Many recent translations steer away from the traditional use of the word 'flesh' (as AV) and use the expression 'sinful nature' (e.g. NIV) or such equivalents. It is felt that 'flesh' may imply in its English usage that the body is somehow intrinsically evil.

[2] See comments about Paul's marital status in Chapter 1.

if you could have done so, you would have torn out your eyes and given them to me' (Galatians 4:15). At the end of his epistle to the Galatians he adds a personal postscript: 'See what large letters I use as I write to you with my own hand!' (Galatians 6:11). It may be that these 'large letters' were necessitated by poor sight.

Although Paul is ambiguous as to the precise nature of his thorn, he is unambiguous as to its origin: it was 'a messenger of Satan, to torment me'. It was satanic in origin and crippling in its effect, so Paul responded in a way most of us would find obvious and commendable: 'I pleaded with the Lord to take it away from me' (v. 8). He did this three times, suggesting not three occasions of prayer, but three periods of time in which he didn't just casually ask for its removal, but pleaded with God to take it away. Paul could probably marshal many reasons why this was not only a reasonable thing for God to do, but a compelling need considering the unique role he exercised in the developing spread of the gospel.

Weakness is strength

God's answer was clear and concise: 'My grace is sufficient for you, for my power is made perfect in weakness.' God stated a vested interest in Paul's weakness, for it would be in his weakness that God would demonstrate his power. There would be but one legitimate explanation for the remarkable ministry of Paul, and it would not be the strength of his personality, his many gifts, his stamina, his evangelistic strategies, his eloquence or his remarkable leadership qualities, all of which he possessed, but the exhibition of the power of God in an obviously weak and weakened vessel.

Sometimes our perceived qualifications for a task become our disqualifications and our perceived disqualifications are the very issues that qualify and equip us for the task. As Hanani the prophet said long before to King Asa in Judah, 'For the eyes of the LORD run to and fro throughout the whole earth, to shew himself strong in the behalf of them whose heart is perfect toward him' (2 Chronicles 16:9 AV). God is not looking for people who are intrinsically strong, but for those who will allow God to show himself strong on their behalf. It is only out of a recognized sense of our innate weakness that this can ever be the case.

Paul talked most intensely about this demonstration of God's power in human weakness in his letters to the Corinthians, and for good reason. The church in Corinth was constituted, in the main, by people from the lower classes who carried little status in society and had little to commend them in worldly terms. Paul addressed them in his first epistle, 'Not many of you were wise by human standards; not many were influential; not many were of noble birth' (1 Corinthians 1:26), and he later implied a number were slaves: 'Were you a slave when you were called? Don't let it trouble you – although if you can gain your freedom, do so' (1 Corinthians 7:21). Corinth had been a city of ruins for a little over a century until Julius Caesar rebuilt it as a Roman colony in 44 BC. It quickly grew in size and rose to become the foremost commercial centre in southern Greece, becoming the seat of the region's proconsul in 27 BC and an imperial province 42 years later in AD 15.

Corinth received a rapid influx of people from around Greece and beyond, soon replacing Antioch as the third city of the empire after Rome and Alexandria. Most of the immigrants were of the lower socio-economic classes, with a large contingent of 'freedmen' from Rome whose status was just above that of a slave. Because there were no landed aristocracy in Corinth, class distinction was based on wealth rather than birth. Corinth, as a coastal port and a busy hub of commerce, was evidently renowned for its vice and especially for its sexual corruption. The term 'Corinthian girl' became a euphemism for a prostitute. It is little wonder, considering the vice and corruption often associated with such a city, that Paul had to deal with issues like sexual immorality (1 Corinthians 5), lawsuits among believers (1 Corinthians 6), idolatry (1 Corinthians 8), gluttony and drunkenness (1 Corinthians 11) when writing to them, for these were the normal features of the prevailing culture, and many of the believers apparently remained gripped by them.

The Corinthian Christians may well have felt socially and academically handicapped, though Paul assured them, 'For we were all baptised by one Spirit into one body – whether Jews or Greeks, slave or free – and we were all given the one Spirit to drink' (1 Corinthians 12:13). They now had a new sense of identity and should live in such a way as to express their incorporation into Christ and the indwelling presence of his Spirit. Their strength, their wisdom, their honour did not derive from what they were in themselves, but by what Jesus Christ could be in them by his Spirit:

> But God chose the foolish things of the world to shame the wise; God chose the weak things of the world to shame the strong. He chose the lowly things of this world and the despised things – and the things that are not – to nullify the things that are, so that no-one may boast before him. It is because of him that you are in Christ Jesus, who has become for us wisdom from God – that is, our righteousness, holiness and redemption. Therefore, as it is written: 'Let him who boasts boast in the Lord.' (1 Corinthians 1:27–31)

Their ground for boasting is exclusively in Jesus Christ who *is* their life, who *is* their strength, who *is* their wisdom, who *is* their righteousness, who *is* their holiness and who *is* their redemption. Jesus Christ has not simply given them these things, but *is* these things in them.

We talk a lot about wholeness today, and very little about brokenness, yet it is our brokenness that qualifies us for effective service, and it is in brokenness that we become whole. Again and again in Scripture, God's interests are best served in people who have come to despair of themselves. Paul stands in a long line of biblical heroes who discovered divine strength in human weakness.

After his upbringing in the Egyptian palace of Pharaoh, 'Moses was educated in all the wisdom of the Egyptians and was powerful in speech and action' (Acts 7:22) and considered himself, for good reason, the obvious and best equipped candidate to lead Israel from its bondage in Egypt to a new life in Canaan: 'Moses thought that his own people would realise that God was using him to rescue them, but they did not' (Acts 7:25). He killed one Egyptian and instead of leading the nation triumphantly from Egypt, Moses found himself a fugitive in the Midian desert for the next 40 years. When God appeared to the 80-year-old Moses in the burning bush, and told him he was sending him back to Egypt to lead the people out of bondage, the old man's reply was, 'Who am I, that I should go to Pharaoh and bring the Israelites out of Egypt?' (Exodus 3:11). That is a markedly different response from the one 40 years earlier when Moses wondered why others failed to recognize him as the saviour of Israel! At 40 he was self-assured, confident of his credentials and competent in his abilities. At the burning bush he is a broken man, aware only of his powerless life, wasted years and apparent disqualification from any use to God. God's response is simply 'I will be with you' (Exodus 3:12). That is all. The events of the next 40 years are not going to be the work of a strong Moses showing his strength for God; instead, they are going to be explicable solely in terms of a strong God working through a weak Moses.

Likewise, Gideon feels crushed and disqualified as he views

the oppression of his people by the Midianite armies who have ruthlessly destroyed the Israelites' crops, killed their livestock and humiliated the people. The angel of the Lord commissions him to act as the mighty warrior of Israel, but Gideon's reply is, 'But Lord . . . how can I save Israel? My clan is the weakest in Manasseh, and I am the least in my family' (Judges 6:15). Everything about Gideon disqualifies him for the task. How does the Lord reply? Exactly as he had to Moses: 'I will be with you' (Judges 6:16). More than that, earlier the Lord had said to Gideon, 'Go in *the strength you have* and save Israel out of Midian's hand' (Judges 6:14, my emphasis). The strength you *have*? 'What strength? I have no strength!' was Gideon's response. The angel of the Lord said to him, 'The LORD is with you, mighty warrior' (Judges 6:12). The strength Gideon has is the strength of God himself.

The weaker we are, the more ready we are to rely on divine strength rather than our own human skills and ingenuity. That is why God waited 40 years until Moses would say, 'Who am I?' At that point the very issue Moses considered his disqualification for the task was to become the essential qualification for the task – his readiness to turn from his own ability to rely entirely on the strength and power of God. God allowed the Midianites to harass and humiliate the Israelites for seven weary years until Gideon could ask 'How can I save Israel? My clan is the weakest . . . I am the least . . . '

We could speak of many others, like the writer of Hebrews who catalogued a long list of men and women through the history of God's dealings with people, 'whose weakness was turned to strength' (Hebrews 11:34). In spiritual life weakness *is* strength, if and when in that weakness we learn to depend entirely and without reserve on God who becomes our strength (see Exodus 15:2; Psalm 28:7; Psalm 118:14; Isaiah 12:2; Habakkuk 3:19). We can never be too weak for God, but we may be too strong for him. We can never be too simple for God, but we may be too clever for him. We can never be too poor for God, but we may be too rich for him. That is why God says to Jeremiah:

> Let not the wise man boast of his wisdom
>> or the strong man boast of his strength
>> or the rich man boast of his riches,
> but let him who boasts boast about this:
>> that he understands and knows me,
>> that I am the LORD . . . (Jeremiah 9:23–24)

Through his own tears of frustration and pleading with God to remove what Paul considered a handicap to his effectiveness, he discovered it was not his *ability* on which God depended, but his *availability*, and sometimes it is our ability that gets in the way and blocks our availability. In order to get our availability, God sometimes has to crush our innate sense of ability. This is not being cruel, but is being kind! Human beings are tempted to overcome, disguise and replace their weaknesses.

When Paul learned to say, 'I will boast all the more gladly about my weaknesses,' he was expressing the paradoxical truth 'so that Christ's power may rest on me . . . For when I am weak, then I am strong' (2 Corinthians 12:9–10).

13

Learning the Secret of Being Content

If you met someone who claimed to have learned to be content whatever their circumstances, you would possibly be a little cynical in your response. If you believed them at all, it is likely you would conclude they had a fairly straightforward life without too many difficulties or hurts.

But this is the exact claim of Paul in his letter to the Philippians. In fact, he repeats the claim twice, adding the second time, 'I have *learned the secret* of being content in any and every situation' (Philippians 4:12, my emphasis). This sense of content-ment was not something instinctive, or to be explained primarily in terms of Paul's personality and temperament; it was a *secret* he had to *learn*, and therefore a secret we too may learn.

The context in which Paul makes that statement is an impor-tant one. The letter to the Philippians presents something of a paradox on first reading. On the one hand it is one of the most positive books in the New Testament. Some 20 times Paul uses words like *rejoice* (9 times); *joy* (8 times); *glad* (3 times) and there is a spirit of confidence and joy that permeates the letter. Perhaps we would be tempted to think on reading it for the first time that Paul is in high spirits, writing from a great location and clearly having a good time. Maybe he has gone on another missionary journey and has ended up on a beautiful semi-tropical island like Malta or Majorca, and is sitting under the shade of a palm tree, toe in the water, dictating to Epaphroditus who is sitting under the next palm tree, 'Rejoice in the Lord always. I will say it again: Rejoice!' (Philippians 4:4). But we could hardly be further from the truth!

The other theme running through the letter is suffering. Four times in the first chapter he speaks of being in 'chains' (see 1:7; 1:13; 1:14; 1:17). He is in chains because he is in prison. He doesn't tell us where he is in prison, but it is almost certainly in Rome. He was imprisoned at least four times in the book of Acts: in Philippi (Acts 16), briefly in Jerusalem (Acts 21–23), for two years in Caesarea (Acts 23–25), taken as a prisoner from Caesarea and shipwrecked on Malta for three months while en route to Rome (Acts 27–28), and finally for two years in Rome itself (Acts 28) where the book of Acts abruptly ends. We have no record of the release of Paul from his Roman imprisonment following the ending of the book of Acts, but tradition affirms fairly confidently that he was released and engaged in another period of missionary activity before being arrested and imprisoned in Rome for a second time. If this is true, it was during his second imprisonment in Rome that Paul wrote to Timothy, much later than the timing of his letter to the Philippians. In his letter to Timothy he commends Onesiphorus for searching him out during an earlier imprisonment:

> May the Lord show mercy to the household of Onesiphorus, because he often refreshed me and was not ashamed of my chains. On the contrary, when he was in Rome, he searched hard for me until he found me. (2 Timothy 1:16–17)

There are different opinions about the location of Paul's imprisonment when he wrote to the Philippians, but almost certainly he was in Rome, not the least evidence being his writing, 'All the saints send you greetings, especially those who belong to Caesar's household' (Philippians 4:22). If he is sending the greetings of the saints in Caesar's household, it doesn't take much intelligence to suppose that he is writing from Rome! If Paul is writing during the imprisonment described at the end of the book of Acts, as is most likely, then we know something of the detail of how he came to be there, and this information adds substance to our understanding of how he has learned to be content.

The circumstances of Paul's arrest

When Paul returned from his third missionary journey he called in on the church in Jerusalem on his way to Antioch, where he was warned that there were thousands of Jewish believers who had remained zealous for the law and who had been informed that Paul was encouraging people to turn away from the law of Moses. There was some partial truth to this rumour in that it was well known Paul had campaigned for an understanding that justification was by faith alone, apart from obedience to the law of Moses. The elders advised Paul that as they had four men who were taking a vow, he should join in their purification rites, pay their expenses and in so doing demonstrate that he was not against Moses, as was rumoured. Paul agreed to this and spent the seven days it took to complete the requirements of the vow.

Towards the end of the seven days, however, he was seen in the temple by some people, who supposed he had brought his Gentile friend, Trophimus, who had accompanied him to Jerusalem from Ephesus, into the temple area where Gentiles were forbidden to go. This was simply not the case, but the rumour quickly spread and a crowd gathered to await Paul's exit from the temple. He was seized and some Jews attempted to kill him; the whole city erupted into chaos. The commander of the Roman troops quickly came on the scene, identified Paul as the source of the trouble, and arrested him. Paul asked for permission to address the crowd that had formed. When he told them he had been sent to preach to the Gentiles, however, the crowd reacted in fury and attempted again to kill him. The commander directed him to be flogged, but as a Roman citizen Paul was able to appeal successfully against this, and was imprisoned for the night. The next day he was brought before the Sanhedrin, and more uproar ensued so Paul was returned to prison. A group of more than 40 men then resolved not to eat until they had killed him, and news of this plot was brought to Paul by his nephew, who also informed the commander.

For Paul's own safety he was then sent to Caesarea, the headquarters of the Roman governor of Judea, with an armed detachment of some 470 soldiers, horsemen and spearmen. In Caesarea he was brought before the governor, Felix, who recognized that there was no case to answer before Roman law and was willing to release him for a bribe. Paul refused to pay any bribe, so he languished in the Caesarean jail for two years before Felix was recalled to Rome and replaced by Festus. Festus wanted to clear the outstanding cases in his prison and heard Paul. But the apostle appealed above the governor's head to Caesar, which as a Roman citizen he had the right to do.

Festus then made arrangements for Paul to be taken to Rome, a journey of many months. The prisoners would sail initially in rough seas to Myra where they would change boats and board an Alexandrian ship sailing to Italy. The ship had a hazardous journey from the start and eventually got caught in a hurricane off Crete. The next 14 days it drifted damaged and out of control until it finally came to grief in the Adriatic Sea when the sailors ran the ship on to a sand bank. What remained was broken to pieces by the pounding of the surf, just off the shore of Malta, to which most of the crew and passengers escaped. They arrived on the island clinging either to planks or to broken pieces of the ship, and spent three months there before getting another boat at the end of winter. This was heading for Italy, and Paul eventually landed in Puteoli on the Italian coast before completing the journey to Rome by land.

Once in Rome, Paul found that Caesar, quite predictably, was not interested in him and the book of Acts finishes with Paul spending two years detained in Rome. For some of this time he was under house arrest with a measure of freedom, and for the rest of it clearly in prison chained to Roman guards. Paul's prison epistles were probably written during this period.

Altogether, something like five years had passed since his arrest in Jerusalem. Two years were spent in Caesarea, two years in Rome, and many additional months on the journey between Caesarea and Rome. From every human perspective these were five wasted years! Paul was in the prime of life. He could have fulfilled his ambition to take the gospel to a new region, to Spain (see Romans 15:23–29), but instead, deprived of his freedom he is languishing for most of that time as a prisoner of imperial Rome.

Rejoicing in tribulation

When his letter from Rome arrived in Philippi, the people there may well have expected to find an angry, disappointed and bitter man writing. After all, it was not the enemies of the gospel who put him there (that might have been quite easy to come to terms with), but the whole fiasco had begun with gossip among believers in Jerusalem who had misunderstood his attitude to the law, who should have known better, and who created the circumstances for his arrest.

Instead of expressions of bitterness they read words like 'Rejoice in the Lord always. I will say it again [just in case they had misunderstood him]: Rejoice!' (Philippians 4:4). How can he write and think like this? We need to keep in mind that this letter is not written in an ivory tower, nor is it a treatise on the theology of joy written at the apostolic desk – theoretical, idealistic but unrelated to real life! This is a man in a Roman prison, chained to guards, deprived of his freedom, wasting the best years of his life, yet discovering the utter sufficiency of Christ and getting excited about it.

This is the kind of man some of us perhaps need to get to know. We may not know the confinement of a Roman cell, but we may experience our own set of chains that restricts us and seems to hinder our sense of usefulness and fulfilment. We may feel the frustration many mothers experience of being 'chained to the kitchen sink', willingly but at some cost too. We may be imprisoned in a marriage that is not working, or perhaps in a job we would love to get out of if it were possible. We may be imprisoned in the tedious and soul-destroying routine of not having a job at all. We may live in a body that is disabled, or be confined in a financial prison, in a situation of loneliness, or one of acute disappointment. We may, like Paul himself, be the victim of gossip and misunderstanding.

The point is this: Paul is writing from his prison cell and saying unambiguously that there are resources for life and even for joy, no matter what our circumstances are, and no matter what our restrictions may be. 'I have learned the secret,' he says, and that secret taught him how to be 'content in any and every situation, whether well fed or hungry, whether living in plenty or in want' (Philippians 4:12).

Learning the secret

What is that secret? Paul suggests to the Philippians two aspects to this. First, he talks about how to survive *internally* – that is, in the inner world of his mind and heart – and secondly, he talks about how to survive *externally* – that is, in the actual circumstances designed from every human perspective to be so troublesome to him.

How to survive internally (Philippians 4:4–7)

The most important thing about any of us is not so much what is happening *to* us as what is happening *in* us. Paul gives a simple formula to help us through the traumas of a troubled heart and inner life:

> Do not be anxious about anything, but in everything, by prayer and petition, with thanksgiving, present your requests to God. And the peace of God, which transcends all understanding, will guard your hearts and your minds in Christ Jesus. (Philippians 4:6–7)

This sounds great of course, but seems completely unreasonable! How can we in the real world with all its possible trials and traumas 'not be anxious about anything'? It almost sounds a neglect of responsibility!

Paul tells us what to do with our anxieties, for have them we certainly will. In any situation that would normally create anxiety, present it to God 'with thanksgiving'. That does not mean we thank God *for* the situation, for there may be many situations about which there is nothing to thank God, but rather we are to thank God *in* the situation for his complete and utter sufficiency and sovereignty, no matter what is happening. Our cause of thankfulness is not the circumstances that cause the anxiety, for that would be absurd, but God who is bigger than any set of circumstances. Our security has to move from being based on our circumstances (for which there is no guaranteed security) to being based in God himself. Paul writes to the Thessalonians, 'Give thanks in all circumstances, for this is God's will for you in Christ Jesus' (1 Thessalonians 5:18). This allows for no exception, for there is no situation in which we may not thank God for his presence and sufficiency.

A key to inner security and stability in the Christian life is a disposition of thankfulness to God – what Stuart Briscoe has called the 'gratitude attitude'. Writing to the Colossians, Paul says, 'And whatever you do, whether in word or deed, do it all in the name of the Lord Jesus, *giving thanks* to God the Father through him' (Colossians 3:17, my emphasis). To be thankful is to express dependency on the one to whom we are being thankful. The most important thing about any of us is where we place our dependency. If our dependency is placed on our circumstances working out as we would like them to, we will inevitably have times of anxiety, for we have no guarantees of any outcome. If our dependency is on God, then our security does not depend on the circumstances of our lives. In fact, it does not matter what they are, for our true sense of security is unrelated to them. Instead of experiencing panic when things go wrong there is, as Paul explains, 'the peace of God, which transcends all understanding'. It is not a rational peace, for it transcends understanding, but it is the peace of God that 'will guard your hearts and your minds in Christ Jesus'. It will serve as the umpire of our emotions and fears and, in the midst of the most traumatic of circumstances, give us that settled sense of security and peace.

Many years ago there was a painting competition held in which the subject to be painted was 'Peace'. There were two prizewinners. One had gone to the English Lake District and painted a beautiful picture on a warm summer day of a lake in the foreground and a mountain range in the background. There was a tranquillity to the scene and the picture made you want to be there and enjoy its calm beauty. He called his picture 'Peace' and won second prize. The other artist had gone to the south-west corner of England and painted a picture in a storm on the Cornish coast. About a third of the way across the picture a high cliff descended into the rough sea where huge waves lashed the bottom of the cliff and sent their white surf high into the air. The skies were heavy with black clouds, the rain was beating down, a tree on the top of the cliff was pushed to a 45-degree angle as the winds blew in from the Atlantic. The picture made you feel cold and glad to be indoors. Halfway up the cliff was a cleft in the rock. In the cleft was a nest and on the nest was a gull, sitting with its eyes closed. The artist called his picture 'Peace' and won first prize.

The peace of God that passes understanding is not the peace of the tranquil Lake District scene, for that does not pass understanding at all. It is entirely reasonable and logical, and what we go looking for when we want some 'peace and quiet'! God does not have to give peace when everything is going well and life is harmonious. Instead, the peace of God is the peace of the Cornish coastal scene, where in the midst of trauma and a howling gale we are at peace in a cleft in the rock, enjoying the security of the sovereignty and sufficiency of the Lord Jesus Christ. This passes understanding; this sets us apart from the neighbours; this enabled Paul not only to survive his circumstances, but to thrive in his years of restriction and imprisonment; this is part of the 'secret of being content in any and every situation'.

But what about the circumstances themselves?

How to survive externally (Philippians 4:10–13)

Paul stresses, 'I know what it is to be in need.' He is not writing a theoretical point but with the authenticity that only comes from first-hand experience in the tough circumstances of life, where the reality of what he affirms has been moulded by hard experience, and he wants the Philippians to know that 'I know'!

> I know what it is to be in need, and I know what it is to have plenty. I have learned the secret of being content in any and every situation, whether well fed or hungry, whether living in plenty or in want. (Philippians 4:12)

He doesn't go into detail here, but we know from other parts of his writings (as mentioned in Chapter 12) that he has had five experiences of being whipped with 39 lashes, he has been beaten with rods, flogged, stoned, left for dead, and imprisoned. He has known acute danger in all sorts of situations, from rivers to bandits, from the antagonism of the Jews, to the hostility of the Gentiles, he has been under threat in the cities and followed in the country, in danger at sea and opposed by false brothers. He has had days without food on his table, and even times without clothes on his back, suffering the endurance of cold and the humiliation of nakedness. He has spent 24 hours in the open rough sea clinging to a part of his sunken ship, and besides all of this he has carried the constant pressure of his concern for his converts and the churches he wants to bring to maturity.

Paul of course knew nothing of the technological advantages we take for granted. His voice was never amplified to make it easier for the crowds to hear. He never recorded a cassette tape or made a radio programme, never got his message out by video or wrote books for mass distribution. He didn't own a car or fly an aeroplane. He travelled on boats that had a tendency to sink! He didn't even send an advance team on his missionary journeys to prepare the local Christians, negotiate with the city authorities, book the central amphitheatre, advertise his meetings and arrive in the city riding the crest of a wave. Once he had arrived, Paul didn't go straight to address large waiting crowds, and when he had completed his planned series of meetings, move on to the next city that had been prepared for him, leaving behind a follow-up team to place the converts in local churches and instruct them further in the things of God! He went on just three missionary journeys as recorded in the book of Acts and possibly one more afterwards, making a total of four journeys in his whole career (as far as we are aware). He often arrived in a city as a stranger, and began at the local synagogue until they inevitably kicked him out. In most cases he ended up as a guest in the local jail, before being persuaded to leave town and move on somewhere else!

In our more comfortable, affluent world we are in great danger of assuming that God is going to look after us a lot better than he did the apostle Paul. If we serve him well, he is somehow obligated to treat us well, so when things do go wrong we question whether we are in the will of God. I suspect that a great many of us would have given up and withdrawn from our ministry had we experienced Paul's difficulties, satisfying ourselves that 'the doors were being closed'.

God has never promised good or easy times to his servants, and Paul knew that through the whole history of God's dealings with humanity it was his best servants who often had the hardest times. Look at the life of Jesus, for example. For 30 years he was never permitted by his heavenly Father to preach a sermon or perform a miracle. He would sit in the synagogue and listen to faulty exposition of the Old Testament Scriptures, but he never interrupted to correct. He would pass a lame man on the road or meet a leper on the street and the best he would do for them was give a loaf of bread or a blanket to keep them warm, but he never healed one of them. At the age of 30 he was baptized by John and the Holy Spirit descended in the form of a dove. Then the Father spoke from heaven: 'This is my Son, whom I love; with him I am well pleased' (Matthew 3:17). This set Jesus apart for his ministry. Never again would he return to his carpenter's shop in Nazareth, but his first assignment was not to go and preach the Sermon on the Mount, or to feed the 5,000, or raise Lazarus from the dead! Instead, 'Then Jesus was led by the Spirit into the desert to be tempted by the devil' (Matthew 4:1). This was his first assignment! Forty days in the desert, with no food, no company and no comfort, with the devil on his back! This was the result of being 'led by the Spirit'. This was not a passport to success and comfort but to conflict and discomfort.

When he eventually preached his first sermon in the synagogue in Nazareth, the crowd's response was not applause but fierce opposition:

> All the people in the synagogue were furious when they heard this. They got up, drove him out of the town, and took him to the brow of the hill on which the town was built, in order to throw him down the cliff. (Luke 4:28–29)

At the end of his first sermon, the whole congregation came forward – but to kill him! They were unsuccessful for 'he walked right through the crowd and went on his way' (Luke 4:30).

For the next three years Jesus' ministry was characterized by open hostility until he was crucified by common consent. Pilate, wishing to release Jesus, put the onus of responsibility on the crowd to pass sentence:

> 'What shall I do, then, with Jesus who is called Christ?' Pilate asked.
>   They all answered, 'Crucify him!'
>   'Why? What crime has he committed?' asked Pilate.
>   But they shouted all the louder, 'Crucify him!'
>
> (Matthew 27:22–23)

Jesus warned his disciples early in his ministry, 'If the head of the house has been called Beelzebub, how much more the members of his household!' (Matthew 10:25). The treatment Jesus had received would be no easier for his servants, and there are no grounds at all on which to expect otherwise.

The realism of Acts

We are in danger sometimes of reading the book of Acts through rose-tinted glasses. We see the tremendous growth of the church, the marvellous demonstrations of power as the Holy Spirit is poured out and released through his people, and we become nostalgic for a return to those early days! But do not overlook the dark side of the book of Acts. In 22 of the 28 chapters of Acts, there is active persecution (and three of the six chapters where there is no persecution include the first three chapters before things had the chance to heat up!). Do not ignore the pain, the humiliation, the suffering, the tears and the premature deaths that are part of the story of the book of Acts.

Stephen, apart from the apostles, was the brightest star in the Jerusalem church. He was the first Christian martyr, and as he was being stoned to death in Jerusalem Luke tells us in Acts:

> But Stephen, full of the Holy Spirit, looked up to heaven and saw the glory of God, and Jesus standing at the right hand of God. 'Look,' he said, 'I see heaven open and the Son of Man standing at the right hand of God.' (Acts 7:55–56)

Jesus is normally seated at the right hand of the Father, but here he is standing. Some have said he is standing to welcome home the first martyr, which may be so. The point I would make, however, is that although Jesus appears as an onlooker of this event he does nothing to prevent the cruel crushing blows of the stones as Stephen slowly dies.

James was the first of the twelve apostles to be executed (in Acts 12), and tradition suggests that all the apostles, with the sole exception of John, died prematurely as martyrs for the Lord Jesus Christ. This was Paul's world, and he did not begrudge the sacrifices that had to be made. In fact it is in this world, with these circumstances, that he states, 'I have learned the secret of being content in any and every situation' (Philippians 4:12). What exactly is the secret?

Paul's answer is, 'I can do everything through him who gives me strength' (Philippians 4:13). This does not mean he can literally do anything – 'I can jump over the moon through Christ' – for this verse has a context and should not be isolated from that context. He is saying, 'I can live within my circumstances – within any circumstance – through Christ who gives me strength.' For every place in which God has put him, Christ is his sufficiency. For every task God has given him, Christ is his strength. For every circumstance that takes him by surprise, Christ is his wisdom. When his back is against the wall, Christ is his security. When this is true, nothing else troubles him. His circumstances become almost irrelevant when his security and sufficiency are in Christ.

Knocked down but never knocked out

Paul writes to the Corinthians:

> But we have this treasure in jars of clay to show that this all-surpassing power is from God and not from us. We are hard pressed on every side, but not crushed; perplexed, but not in despair; persecuted, but not abandoned; struck down, but not destroyed. We always carry around in our body the death of Jesus, so that the life of Jesus may also be revealed in our body. For we who are alive are

always being given over to death for Jesus' sake, so that his life may
be revealed in our mortal body. (2 Corinthians 4:7–11)

He is saying that it is true we are hard pressed, but we are never
crushed. It is true we are perplexed, and scratch our heads in
confusion many times, but we are never in despair. It is true we
are persecuted and wonder if we can bear the pain of it, but we
are never abandoned. It is true we are struck down and sometimes wonder if we will ever get on our feet again, but we are not
destroyed. One paraphrase of this passage says, 'We are
knocked down but never knocked out.' Why did Paul experience
such brutality? Here is one reason he gives, 'For we who are alive
are always being given over to death for Jesus' sake, *so that his
life may be revealed in our mortal body*' (2 Corinthians 4:11, my
emphasis). Paul's sufferings provide another opportunity for the
life of Jesus to be seen and revealed in him. When there is a
natural explanation for the way we act and react to circumstances it reveals nothing of Christ, but when we respond as
Paul responded our lives become an exhibition of Christ.

Is this the Jesus we know – the Jesus who enables us to live in
any circumstance and carry any burden? Or do we have a Jesus
who is little more than the patron of our Christianity? Do we
live it in his name, try to keep up with his teaching and seek to
imitate his lifestyle, but know little or nothing of his supernatural intervention and 'the peace of God which transcends all
understanding'?

What exactly is the 'secret' Paul claims to have learned? It is
not the secret of how to get God to take us out of our circumstances (that is often what we look for and the frequent object
of our prayers), but the secret of how to bring God in to our
circumstances! That is what makes the difference. This is where
we experience his peace and contentment.

Have you learned this secret yet?

14

Passing the Baton

The book of Acts finishes rather abruptly with Paul under house arrest in Rome, enjoying a measure of freedom in his own rented house where 'boldly and without hindrance he preached the kingdom of God and taught about the Lord Jesus Christ' (Acts 28:31). As to why the book ends so abruptly, or what happened next, we may only speculate. Did Luke record the 'two whole years' (Acts 28:30) of Paul's Roman imprisonment after they had finished, implying he was released afterwards? Or did Luke die around this time while Paul was still a prisoner, and the time period was added by an editor to finish the story, but with no further details?

Paul's release from this Roman imprisonment is most probable for, as has been stated, 'the prison epistles expect it, the pastoral epistles demand it, and tradition asserts it'. We may concur with those three points. If Paul wrote his prison epistles during his Roman imprisonment, as is likely, he was certainly anticipating release in due course. He writes to the Philippians, 'I know that through your prayers and the help given by the Spirit of Jesus Christ, what has happened to me will turn out for my deliverance' (Philippians 1:19), and writing to Philemon about his returning runaway slave Onesimus he asks him to,

'Prepare a guest room for me, because I hope to be restored to you in answer to your prayers' (Philemon 22). Freedom was clearly Paul's expectation at the time of writing.

Writing later to Timothy, Paul seems to be referring to his release from Caesar when he states:

> At my first defence, no-one came to my support, but everyone deserted me. May it not be held against them. But the Lord stood at my side and gave me strength, so that through me the message might be fully proclaimed and all the Gentiles might hear it. And I was delivered from the lion's mouth. (2 Timothy 4:16–17)

His 'first defence' almost certainly refers to his defence before Caesar, rather than to his defence in Jerusalem several years before when he was first arrested, for he did have his supporters in Jerusalem. Paul had been told by an angel, on the journey to Rome, 'Do not be afraid, Paul. You must stand trial before Caesar' (Acts 27:24), so stand before Caesar he would have done, though clearly sometime after the book of Acts concludes, for Luke makes no reference to an actual trial. His statement 'I was delivered from the lion's mouth' may well refer to the fact that he was found not guilty of the charges against him and released from prison.

Two years after Rome

There is evidence from the pastoral epistles that Paul, once released in Rome, continued his ministry for around two more years. We may only speculate about his movements during that time, but there are one or two clues about some possible movements. He had requested lodging in the home of Philemon in Colosse when he sent his letter with the returning slave Onesimus, so he may well have gone to Colosse in Asia Minor having not previously visited that city, although he had corresponded with the church there. He reminds Timothy in his first letter to him:

> As I urged you when I went into Macedonia, stay there in Ephesus so that you may command certain men not to teach false doctrines any longer nor to devote themselves to myths and endless genealogies. These promote controversies rather than God's work – which is by faith. (1 Timothy 1:3)

This would indicate Paul had visited Ephesus and from there had travelled on to Macedonia. In concluding his second letter to Timothy – the final letter we have that he wrote – he mentions having recently been in Corinth and Miletus. To Titus he writes, 'The reason I left you in Crete was that you might straighten out what was left unfinished and appoint elders in every town, as I directed you' (Titus 1:5). Paul had visited Crete on his first missionary journey with Barnabas many years before, but this more recent visit must have followed his release from prison in Rome. Various traditions also suggest a journey west from Rome that, if it did in fact take place, would almost certainly have included Spain.

Whatever the facts about Paul's release and movements following the conclusion of the book of Acts, it was only for a matter of around two years that he again enjoyed his itinerant ministry, before he came to an untimely end in the great persecution of Christians initiated by Nero in Rome in the year AD 64, the traditional date for Paul's death. Paul's final letter to Timothy is again written from prison, but unlike letters from his earlier imprisonment, in this letter he does not anticipate regaining his freedom:

> For I am already being poured out like a drink offering, and the time has come for my departure. I have fought the good fight, I have finished the race, I have kept the faith. Now there is in store for me

the crown of righteousness, which the Lord, the righteous Judge, will award to me on that day – and not only to me, but also to all who have longed for his appearing. (2 Timothy 4:6–8)

It is most likely he died soon after this, as one of the many Christian martyrs in Rome that year.

Persecution in Rome

In the year AD 64, two years after the end of the book of Acts, there was a great fire in the city of Rome. It raged for five days and did enormous damage, completely destroying five of the 14 districts into which the city was divided and severely damaging another seven, leaving only two untouched. Rumour had it that Nero instigated the fire, because he had let it be known he wanted to rebuild much of the city to his personal specifications. Rebuilding was not a popular idea with the people, as it would involve destroying homes and businesses before any reconstruction could take place and would inevitably involve displacing many of the city's inhabitants in the process. Whether or not there was any truth in this rumour, Nero began to look for scapegoats. What class of people within the city could he instigate strong suspicion and hostility towards? He found his answer in the Christians. The historian Tacitus is one of our most reliable sources for these events and he records:

Therefore, to scotch the rumour, Nero substituted as culprits and punished with the utmost refinements of cruelty, a class of men, loathed for their vices, whom the crowd styled Christians . . . First of all, those who confessed were arrested; then on their information a huge multitude was convicted, not so much on the ground of incendiarism as for the hatred of the human race. Their execution was made a matter of sport: some were sewn up in the skins of wild beasts and savaged to death by dogs; others were fastened to crosses as living torches, to serve as lights when daylight failed. Nero made his gardens available for the show, and held games in the Circus, mingling with the crowd or standing in his chariot in his charioteer's uniform.[1]

To justify this wave of persecution, all kinds of malicious ideas were distributed about Christians, including, among many other things, that they were guilty of cannibalism (eating the flesh and drinking the blood of Christ), of gross acts of sexual immorality (their 'love feasts' were said to be sexual orgies), and that they were political revolutionaries plotting to overthrow the Roman Empire by preaching a kingdom superior to Rome, the kingdom of God. It is fairly certain that Paul was among those who perished in that first wave of persecution. Persecutions continued on and off in the Roman Empire for almost 250 years until the conversion of the Emperor Constantine in AD 312.

Encouraging timid Timothy

Paul's impending martyrdom makes his second letter to Timothy particularly poignant. He is anticipating his imminent death and is passing the baton to a new generation. His trust in Timothy is expressed against a background of a list of people who have fallen away from Christ, amounting to a landslide in Asia: 'You know that everyone in the province of Asia has deserted me, including Phygelus and Hermogenes' (2 Timothy 1:15). Later he laments that 'Demas, because he loved this world, has deserted me and has gone to Thessalonica. Crescens has gone to Galatia, and Titus to Dalmatia . . . Alexander the

---

[1] Quoted by F.F. Bruce, *Paul: Apostle of the Heart Set Free* (Eerdmans, 1979), p. 442.

metalworker did me a great deal of harm' (2 Timothy 4:10–14). With so much falling away, and with the ease with which former colleagues seemed to depart from the truth, it was imperative for the truth to be both 'guarded' (1:14) and 'preached' (4:2).

Timothy would not be seen as a natural successor to Paul. He was clearly a very different personality: timid, withdrawing, and with a tendency to fear. Paul encourages him to 'fan into flame the gift of God, which is in you' (2 Timothy 1:6), to 'not be ashamed to testify about our Lord' (1:8), and to 'be strong in the grace that is in Christ Jesus' (2:1), all implying the tendency to hold back and withdraw. The strength for the task he is being entrusted with will come from 'the grace that is in Christ Jesus', but this is not just passively received – he must be strong, disciplined and unashamed.

Paul had boldly asserted to the Philippians, 'Whatever you have learned or received or heard from me, or seen in me – put it into practice' (Philippians 4:9). He set himself in that instance as an example to be followed in two particular areas: what has been 'heard from me' he urges them to keep, and what has been 'seen in me' he urges them to do. These two issues are repeated in his second letter to Timothy as areas where Paul the elder missionary statesman is to be an example to his young lieutenant as he passes the torch. He is to guard the truth he has heard from Paul, and he is to follow the pattern he has seen in Paul.

What you have heard from me – keep!

First, he says 'What you heard from me, keep as the pattern of sound teaching' (2 Timothy 1:13). To Paul truth was not a personal possession but a revelation whose content must be guarded and distributed at all cost, 'in season and out of season' (4:2). He tells Timothy: 'Guard the good deposit that was entrusted to you – guard it with the help of the Holy Spirit who lives in us' (1:14). To Paul, the gospel was not a matter of opinion, to be held above other opinions, but a matter of objective truth that was non-negotiable. By definition, truth is timeless and unchanging. It may at times be forgotten, neglected, perverted, opposed, rejected, counterfeited or displaced, but it never changes. The truth Paul proclaimed was not merely an emphasis he stressed, a concept to titillate the mind, a particular party line or an option to be agreed or disputed at will, but by its very nature an imperative to which there has to be a response.

Paul's message centred on the person and work of Jesus Christ, making it much more than a series of theological propositions, or articles of a creed. These may be helpful to our understanding and necessary for our good, but they do not in themselves constitute the truth; they simply point to it. The truth is the person and activity of Jesus, who did not say, 'I teach the truth', or 'I reveal the truth', but '*I am* the truth'. All that is theologically true, is truth about Jesus, and to embrace the truth is to allow that which is true of Jesus to become true of us. This is the heart and substance of the gospel that is to be both guarded and proclaimed. It concerns the person of Christ.

It is important to affirm that Scripture is true and without error in all that it declares, for it is inspired by the Holy Spirit, and is given to us for our benefit, and is to be completely trusted. The Scriptures, however, are not in themselves the truth. A train timetable may be true, but it is not the truth. A train timetable plays a vital role in telling us how to get from point A to point B and when to travel, but is incapable of taking us anywhere itself! If a timetable is true, it is so only because it bears witness to the truth – the train. The timetable tells us about the activity of the train so that we may understand it, get on board and enjoy the ride. Scripture is true, but in itself will not do us any good if detached from Christ. It is true only as it bears witness to the truth and brings us to Christ, so that we may become the recipients of his life and enjoy all the benefits of his work for us, in us and through us.

The apostle Paul in his day did not have a Bible to leave with his converts – he could only leave them Christ. He explains his follow-up strategy to the Philippians when he writes:

> In all my prayers for all of you, I always pray with joy . . . being confident of this, that he who began a good work in you will carry it on to completion until the day of Christ Jesus. (Philippians 1:4–6)

Who began the good work in them? Christ. Who will carry it on to completion? Christ. Christ was not the patron of Paul's Christianity, the one in whose name it was to be lived. Christ was the very substance of his gospel, and what he left behind was the presence of the living Jesus in each person who had been brought into union with him. That alone is what made them Christians, and his activity through them is what made them effective.

If Christ is the truth, however, the primary means by which we know him is his word, so the Scriptures are of paramount importance to that end. Paul tells Timothy, 'Do your best to present yourself to God as one approved, a workman who does not need to be ashamed and who correctly handles the word of truth' (2 Timothy 2:15). All we may reliably know of Christ we know through his word, so we have to approach Scripture as a workman approaches his work, with discipline and conscientiousness, not moulding it to preconceived ideas but letting it mould and form us.

The discipline of a workman is similar to Paul's earlier exhortation to Timothy when he tells him he must endure hardship like a soldier, compete like an athlete and work hard like a farmer (2 Timothy 1:3–7). Our understanding of truth is not dependent solely on brain power and concentration, for Timothy is to 'guard the good deposit that was entrusted to you – guard it with the help of the Holy Spirit who lives in us' (1:14). But the Holy Spirit's active participation in the process occurs as we work to understand and grapple with the truth.

What you have seen in me – do!

Paul's second example as he passes the baton to Timothy is in keeping the pattern of godly living his young friend has witnessed in Paul over many years:

> You, however, know all about my teaching, my way of life, my purpose, faith, patience, love, endurance, persecutions, sufferings – what kinds of things happened to me in Antioch, Iconium and Lystra, the persecutions I endured. Yet the Lord rescued me from all of them. (2 Timothy 3:10–11)

This is a list of nine qualities that Timothy has observed in Paul and which he is to emulate. Seven of them are active, and the last two, 'my persecutions and sufferings', are passive. The old saying 'Some things are better caught than taught' applies here. What we see speaks more loudly to us than what we hear. In the old pre-video days of reel-to-reel films, if the soundtrack was not synchronized with the film it was always the soundtrack that was perceived as being too slow or too fast, and never the film. What we see represents reality, and if what we hear does not synchronize with it, then what we hear is subject to question. Paul was both confident and bold enough to assert that what could be seen in his life and behaviour was a model of the truth he proclaimed with his lips, to be imitated by others and regarded as a plumb line for measuring godly attitudes and behaviour.

He not only wrote in this vein to Timothy as he anticipated his own death, but he had earlier written something similar to the Philippians: 'Join with others in following my example, brothers, and take note of those who live according to the pattern we gave you' (Philippians 3:17); and to the Corinthians, 'Follow my example, as I follow the example of Christ' (1 Corinthians 11:1); and to the Thessalonians, 'You became imitators of us and of the Lord' (1 Thessalonians 1:6). This is a man confident, not of his own abilities, for he has declared those to be bankrupt, but of the ability of the Lord Jesus Christ, who had expressed himself in Paul, to do the same in all those who would equally submit themselves to Christ.

The nine things Timothy had seen in Paul and which he encouraged him to imitate were as follows.

1. My teaching

It is most likely Timothy had been converted to Christ as a result of Paul's preaching in Lystra on his first missionary journey (see Acts 14:8–20). Timothy's home was Lystra (see Acts 16:1) and Paul refers to him as 'my true son in the faith' (1 Timothy 1:2; see also 1:18; 2 Timothy 1:2; 2:1), so Paul's teaching has been the basic diet of Timothy's nurture and growth since his conversion. It is a great thing when a person does not have to unlearn some of the teaching they have first been exposed to but, as Paul instructed Timothy, can 'continue in what you have learned and have become convinced of, because you know those from whom you learned it' (2 Timothy 3:14). Timothy now has the responsibility to 'guard . . . with the help of the Holy Spirit who lives in us' (2 Timothy 1:14).

2. My way of life

Timothy had been able to observe at close quarters what it was that made Paul 'tick'. Paul had picked him up in Lystra near the commencement of his second missionary journey and taken him along as a companion and assistant, and Timothy had witnessed Paul during his triumphs and troubles through the next two years or so. You can't hide very much when you live in close proximity with someone for so long. It was said at the memorial service of a missionary statesman some years ago that he was never caught off guard, for the simple reason, he never had to be on guard. What was seen was who he was. Paul never needed to be on guard, so could open his 'way of life' to the scrutiny of those who knew him.

3. My purpose

What motivates a person is one of the most important things about them. Paul states his ultimate ambition to the Philippians:

> I want to know Christ and the power of his resurrection and the fellowship of sharing in his sufferings, becoming like him in his death, and so, somehow, to attain to the resurrection from the dead. (Philippians 3:10–11)

This perspective permeated everything he did, said and lived for.

4. My faith

Paul's teaching on faith is a repeated theme of his letters, to the extent that 'everything that does not come from faith is sin' (Romans 14:23). That which does not derive from a spirit of dependence on God, by definition must derive from a spirit of independence of God, which is the nature of sin. The most important thing about any of us is where we place our dependency, and Paul was unambiguously dependent on Christ.

5. *My patience*

It is probably born out of experience that Paul writes to the Romans, 'Tribulation worketh patience' (Romans 5:3 AV), for no doubt he had learned to be patient through hardships and suffering. Timothy had been with Paul in Philippi when Paul and Silas had been thrown into prison, an earthquake had occurred and the prison doors had flown open. Rather than take the opportunity to escape, Paul and Silas stayed to lead the distressed jailer and his family to Christ. Paul later told the Philippians from his prison in Rome, 'I am put here for the defence of the gospel' (Philippians 1:16). There was no sense of panic or disaster; rather, an explicit trust in the sovereignty of God that resulted in a quiet sense of patience.

6. *My love*

Paul had explained to the Corinthians that without love he would be just 'a resounding gong or a clanging cymbal' (1 Corinthians 13:1). Timothy had himself been the recipient of Paul's love and kindness and had seen its constant expression, without discrimination, to those he served and ministered to.

7. *My endurance*

This is the positive expression of which patience is the more passive aspect, reflecting his response to difficult circumstances in which he not only patiently accepted difficulties, but persevered and endured through them.

8. *My persecutions*

Paul also reminds Timothy of 'what kinds of things happened to me in Antioch, Iconium and Lystra, the persecutions I endured' (2 Timothy 3:11). He refers to these incidents because they surround the time of Timothy's conversion, events that would have created an early and vivid impression on the young man, and of which he would have been a witness. He would have seen the crowd drag Paul outside his home city of Lystra, stone him, and leave him for dead (see Acts 14). He would have known that Paul arrived in Lystra from Iconium where there had also been plots to stone him.

9. My sufferings

These had not just been the prerogative of Paul, for he immediately tells Timothy, 'In fact, everyone who wants to live a godly life in Christ Jesus will be persecuted, while evil men and impostors will go from bad to worse, deceiving and being deceived' (2 Timothy 3:12–13). Persecution and suffering is not going to be a sign of failure or disaster, but an evidence of godliness, and Timothy needs to brace himself for this continuing reality as Paul hands the baton to him.

This is the legacy Paul is leaving Timothy. There is nothing sentimental about it and there are no illusions in Paul's thinking about ease, comfort and prosperity as the birthright of servants of God. On the contrary, serving God involves warfare, struggle and tears. There will be those among the believing community who will

> not put up with sound doctrine. Instead, to suit their own desires, they will gather around them a great number of teachers to say what their itching ears want to hear. They will turn their ears away from the truth and turn aside to myths. (2 Timothy 4:3–4)

Timothy needs to be sure of his ground and take his stand in such circumstances. To stand for truth may not make him popular – even among the people of God who become so easily seduced and diverted.

But there is no sense of panic in Paul as he approaches his

impending death. He has no illusions about his indispensability to God, or to the church, or to the maintenance of the truth, but he is fully convinced of the indispensability of God and his truth to the church and to his servants. This is why the truth must be guarded and preached, and he can willingly place the baton in the hand of a frequently ill and timid Timothy (see 1 Timothy 5:23; 2 Timothy 1:7) – and do so with confidence, knowing his confidence is not in Timothy but in the God who indwells him and will continue to work through him.

We know nothing of the final trial that almost certainly led to Paul's execution in the hysteria of persecution that broke out against the believers in Rome. All the hints suggest that he stood alone at the end, for in his first defence he explains to Timothy, 'No-one came to my support, but everyone deserted me' (2 Timothy 4:16). His only strength came from the Lord, who 'stood at my side and gave me strength' (v. 17). How long he waited for his subsequent and final trial we do not know, but we do know he did so with the conviction that 'the Lord . . . will bring me safely to his heavenly kingdom' (v. 18).

And he did. His deepest desire was finally granted: 'I . . . would prefer to be away from the body and at home with the Lord' (2 Corinthians 5:8).

Study Guide

Chapter 1 Drama on the Damascus road

1. What losses were involved in your conversion that may equate with Paul's, 'For whose sake I have lost all things' (Philippians 3:8)?

2. What are some of the means by which God revealed himself to you?

3. Looking back, what evidences do you see of God drawing you to himself before your actual conversion?

4. Discuss the significant changes that take place in every case of conversion to Christ, whether dramatic like Paul, or unsensational.

Chapter 2 Profile of a convert

1. Saul was persecuting Christians as an expression of his desire to please God. What symptoms do you see in people that may be an expression of a search for God?

2. 'Actions may give a completely conflicting impression to the true attitude of heart.' Discuss situations where you may have seen this.

3. It is intriguing that Paul had several Christian relatives. What part do you think they may have played in his conversion?

4. What difference do you think the discovery that Jesus Christ is *alive* makes to the Christian life?

Chapter 3 Motivated by vision

1. How important has a sense of vision been in your own life?

2. How should we cope with frustrated vision?

3. 'When we ask God to show us his will, we often want him to give us a road map, whereas what he is more likely to give us is a compass' (see page 42.) How do you respond to this statement?

4. What do you think is necessary to reach the goals and visions God puts in our hearts?

Chapter 4 Time out with God

1. Discuss the statement: 'No human being can ever become a substitute for learning from Christ himself' (page 58), and consider the ways in which we practically learn from Christ.

2. How do we guard against 'making things up' about the Christian life that sound and feel good but which are not actually true?

3. How do we today go about 'knowing his will and hearing words from his mouth' (see page 61).

4. Discuss the difference between knowing '*what*' we believe and '*whom*' we believe (see 2 Timothy 1:12).

Chapter 5 The value of a friend

1. The name 'Barnabas' means 'son of encouragement' (see Acts 4:36). Discuss how he lived up to that reputation from the following passages: Acts 4:36–37; Acts 9:26–27; Acts 11:22–26; Acts 15:36. Think of specific people who may need your encouragement in a similar way.

2. When Paul returned to his Jewish context in Tarsus, he may have denied himself the liberty of flaunting his freedom in Christ and placed himself under the requirements of the Jewish law so as not to be a stumbling block to others. In what circumstances is this an appropriate principle for us today?

3. Paul had a long period in Tarsus where he seemed to make no headway spiritually. How should we respond to such times of apparent barrenness in our own lives?

4. What are some practical ways you can encourage others in their growth in God?

Chapter 6 Finding and doing the will of God

1. How does the principle 'We live by faith, not by sight' (2 Corinthians 5:7) apply to the question of guidance and discerning the will of God for our lives?

2. Look up the following verses that state categorically what the will of God is, and discuss how your personal search for guidance should be influenced by them:

   1 Thessalonians 4:3
   1 Thessalonians 5:18
   1 Peter 2:13–15
   1 Peter 4:19

3. What would you consider the three most important criteria in your life in discerning the will of God?

4. How do you think your church could be actively involved in discerning and encouraging the will of God in its members?

Chapter 7 A strategy for evangelism

1. Do you have a strategy for evangelizing your area? If so, what can you learn from Paul to enhance this? If not, how do you think you could go about establishing one?

2. What do you think may be common ground from which you could build a bridge to Christ for your family, neighbours and community?

3. Discuss some positive ways we could respond to people of other faiths without compromising the truth of Jesus Christ.

4. In the light of the last paragraph of the chapter, how far back do you think we need to go today to find a satisfactory starting point in presenting the gospel?

Chapter 8 Restoring righteousness

1. How would you define the gift of an evangelist?

2. Discuss, in the light of this chapter, how people are made aware of their sin. How does this correspond to the realization of your own sinfulness?

3. What is the relationship between law and grace?

4. What does it mean for us to 'live by faith'?

Chapter 9 Facing foolish Christians

1. Discuss the statement, 'Any addition to Christ is by definition a subtraction from him' (page 135).

2. Define, and then discuss, the relationship between justification, sanctification and glorification.

3. What are the stumbling blocks today that cause us to be 'foolish' like the Galatians (see Galatians 3:1–3)?

4. What does Paul mean by 'working out our salvation' (see Philippians 2:12–13)?

Chapter 10 Union with Christ

1. Summarize what it means for the Christian to be in 'union with Christ'.

2. Discuss the implications of the following statement: 'There are two invitations of Jesus in which the whole of the Christian life may be seen to be encompassed. His first invitation is "Come to me" (Matthew 11:28) and his second is "Remain in me" (John 15:4)' (see pages 141–2).

3. Discuss the significance of baptism.

4. What are the practical implications of being 'crucified with Christ' (page 146).

Chapter 11 Civil war in the soul

1. Whom do you consider Romans 7:15–23 to be describing?

2. Discuss the role of the devil and the role of the human heart in temptation and sin.

3. How does the Holy Spirit counteract sin in the life of a Christian?

4. What practical things are we doing (or should we do) to bring about the renewing of our minds?

Chapter 12 The strength of weakness

1. Discuss some of the positive benefits that may come from suffering. How does this equate with Paul's view?

2. Are there some things in your life and circumstances that you would have changed if you could have done so, but which, with hindsight, you now see to be a means of God bringing greater benefits into your life?

3. Discuss the value of the author's statement, 'It is in brokenness that we become whole' (page 174).

4. Why does Paul state 'When I am weak, then I am strong' (2 Corinthians 12:10)?

Chapter 13 Learning the secret of being content

1. Do you think it is right to deny ourselves the negative emotions of anger and bitterness when we have been badly treated? How does Paul's letter to the Philippians relate to your answer?

2. What is the difference between thanking God *for* all circumstances, and thanking God *in* all circumstances?

3. How does God want us to live in difficult circumstances?

4. Discuss the author's statement that the *secret* Paul has learned is not about how to get God to take us out of our circumstances, but for us to bring God into our circumstances (page 191). How should this be applied practically?

Chapter 14 Passing the baton

1. Paul laments, 'Everyone in Asia deserted me' (2 Timothy 1:15). What kind of support and encouragement should we give to our fellow Christians, especially when they are in trouble of some kind?

2. Paul set himself as a model for Timothy to imitate regarding his teaching and lifestyle. Who has been the biggest influence on you, and why?

3. Discuss the statement, 'Scripture is true, but in itself will not do us any good if detached from Christ' (page 199).

4. How does a perspective on heaven help us to cope with difficult situations in life?

Selective Bibliography

F. F. Bruce, *Paul: Apostle of the Free Spirit* (Paternoster, 1977).

F. F. Bruce, *New Testament History* (Thomas Nelson & Sons, 1969).

F. F. Bruce, *The Book of Acts* (Marshall, Morgan & Scott, 1954).

F. F. Bruce, *The Pauline Circle* (Paternoster Press, 1985).

Everett Ferguson, *Backgrounds of Early Christianity* (Eerdmans, 1993).

Geoffrey Grogan, *Wrestling with the Big Issues* (Christian Focus Publications, 1993).

Donald Guthrie, *The Apostles* (Pickering and Inglis, 1975).

Gerald F. Hawthorne, Ralph P. Martin, Daniel G. Reid (eds), *Dictionary of Paul and His Letters* (InterVarsity Press, 1993).

Kevin A. Miller (ed.), 'Paul and His Times', *Christian History*, Issue 47 (Vol. XIV, No 3).

Campbell Morgan, *The Book of Acts* (Pickering and Inglis, 1946).

John Pollock, *Paul: The Apostle* (Kingsway, 1999).

James S. Stewart, *A Man in Christ* (Hodder & Stoughton, 1935).

John R. W. Stott, *The Message of Acts* (InterVarsity Press, 1990).

John R. W. Stott, *The Message of Romans* (InterVarsity Press, 1994).

Index of Life Issues

Page numbers often mark the beginning of a topic that continues for several pages.

Baptism	145	Heaven	74
		Holiness	85
Church	89	Holy Spirit	83, 144, 160
Contentment	177		
Conversion	9	Indwelling Christ	138, 139, 144,
Creation	111		149, 175, 191
Crucifixion with Christ	147		
		Justification	133
Disciplined living	138		
Disposition of heart	24	Law and grace	122, 130
		Laying on of hands	89
Encouragement	76, 197	Legalism	73
Evangelism	97, 113		
		Marriage	14
Faith	123	Mysticism	66
Family	30, 72		
Friendship	69	Obedience	39, 52, 83, 126
Fruit of the Spirit	119, 164		
		Patience	155
Grace	122	Peace	183
Gratitude	87	Persecution	68, 94
Guidance	48, 81		

Regeneration	34	Spirit and word	160
Repentance	162	Suffering	41, 167, 178, 193
Resurrection life	32		
Revelation	19, 60	Union with Christ	141
Righteousness	116		
		Vision	34, 37
Seeking for God	25		
Sin	153	Weakness	127, 151, 167
Solitude	57		

Two books by Charles Price...

Stop Trying to Live for Jesus ...
Let Him Live Through You

How easy it is to come under the burden of attempting the impossible: a life lived in our own strength rather than in the power available to us in Christ.

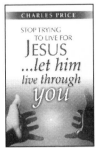

If you want to break out of the cycle of trying, failing and trying again, this book is for you.

Christ in You

Charles Price shows how God's presence, his laws and his daily provision will satisfy us in the frenetic pace of modern life. With clarity and warmth he explains some of the Bible's less well-known symbols, and so awakens us to a whole new understanding of what it is for Christ to live in us.

Kingsway Publications

The Character and Charisma series

ELIJAH: ANOINTED AND STRESSED
by Jeff Lucas
The portrait of a biblical hero who knew power, but not without pain. Jeff Lucas points us to a God who is big enough to help us through days of defeat.

ELISHA: A SIGN AND A WONDER
by Greg Haslam
Lays the emphasis on practical application, using stories to communicate theology in an imaginative, memorable and humorous way.

ESTHER: FOR SUCH A TIME AS THIS
by Jill Hudson
Like many modern-day heroes and media figures, Esther had a role to play that combined a luxurious lifestyle with great personal cost. She discovered her true destiny and purpose in life through the choices that really count, and so can you.

GIDEON: POWER FROM WEAKNESS
by Jeff Lucas
One of the most effective leaders in Israel's history, Gideon's victory over the Midianites was a triumph against the odds. Yet his battle against his own fear and insecurity was the hardest he faced.

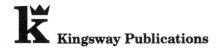 **Kingsway Publications**

The Character and Charisma series

JOSHUA: POWER TO WIN
by Kevin Logan
Joshua spied the land, and saw things in Canaanite society to turn his blood cold. But he also knew what it was to overcome his fears by trusting in a God who had gone before him.

MARY: THE MOTHER OF JESUS
by Wendy Virgo
Mary is the prototype Christian woman. No illusions about herself, no expectations of being special, but ready to do God's will. From the first Christmas to the first Easter and beyond, we follow Mary, the mother of Jesus.

MOSES: THE MAKING OF A LEADER
by Cleland Thom
A clear and biblical exploration of leadership, showing how God trained Moses and made him into one of the greatest leaders – and meekest of men.

SAMSON: THE SECRET OF STRENGTH
by Phil Stanton
What sort of man was Samson? A man of brawn rather than brain – physically strong but morally weak? Yet he is listed among the heroes of faith. Phil Stanton shows the lessons we can learn from his story.

Kingsway Publications